The **10** Percent

How to Unlock God's Blessings and Break the Cycle of Greed

Bishop Luis R. Scott

Columbus, GA

2

Table of Contents

Table of Contents 3

Foreword 5

Introduction 9

Chapter One 13
 Theology of the Tithing

Chapter Two 55
 Origin of the Tithe

Chapter Three 93
 Answering Objections

Conclusion 111

Foreword

What do you do when you discover some new piece of information and it changes everything else you thought you knew? The answer most of us would like to give is, "We adjust." However, the maxim is quite true, no one wants change. Change can be a scary and unsettling proposition. Especially when we are unable to see what happens on the other side of it.

In my almost four decades of life, I have seen firsthand what it looks like for a man to live in the difficult place between God and the world. My father has exemplified a life of integrity, faithfulness, and diligent study. He has done all these things while being a husband, father, soldier, and pastor. Through all of the challenges and successes, he has demonstrated that change is not an enemy. Rather, change is the price we pay to become everything God envisioned in and for us from the foundations of the world.

Along the way, my father has worked to read between the lines, to ask the questions no one was asking, and to hear what people are not saying. Over the course of more than sixty-four trips around the sun, he has learned to trust in God and to keep every appointment God makes for him. Because of his willingness to follow God wherever he leads, change has never been something to fear.

In six decades, it can be difficult to quantify how much can be learned. The problem for many people is that our memories are shorter than our lives are long. So, how do we make sure that we continue to grow? One way is to make sure you are able to mark the passage of time by learning to connect the dots of God's grace. Each of these historical dots punctuate our lives and serve as reminders of God's goodness and faithfulness. In my father's life many of these dots have been codified in little sayings he likes to use.

The power of these sayings are word pictures. They help those who hear them to envision a truth that can be used in daily life. These nuggets of wisdom, the little "secrets" as he likes to call them, have served as both boundaries and guides in my life. As boundaries, I have learned to anticipate and avoid many of the traps to be found in the world. As guides, these littles secrets have helped me to chart my course as I have sought to find my own path in the world.

This book is the latest example of another secret. It is the exposition of a secret God gave to the human race very early on. But, as is the case with many things God reveals, we have missed it. Even though it has been in his Word the entire time. The greatest obstacle to a vibrant faith has never been pain and suffering. It has always been idolatry. Whenever we place our trust in anything more than in the one true God, we become guilty of this activity. As a matter of fact, we should call it what it properly is, it is sin because it is also a form of blasphemy. Giving what properly belongs to God to anything else in our lives is an affront to God's glory.

I know that to some it may sound like overstatement. But I want to assure you that it is not. Even today, two thousand years from the Resurrection of Jesus of Nazareth, we have not heeded the warning. The number of distractions have multiplied with each societal and technological "advance." The numbers of gods vying for the affections of the human race can no longer be counted. But there is one idol that seems to be the favorite of those who claim the name of Christ.

In this book, you will be (re)introduced to the one idol Jesus himself identified as the greatest enemy of the Church. As we look at why this idol is so problematic, we will also be taken behind the curtain to see the tactics of distraction and deception used by the enemy our souls, the devil. Whether we want to admit it or not, the devil wants to entice us to give our worship of God to an unworthy claimant to the throne of our lives.

As you will discover, the power of the tithe is not about getting rich with the wealth of the world. It is about becoming free from the power of sin and greed. The tithe is the one secret God did not wait to reveal to his people but has been more often hidden by his people themselves. We have failed to discern God's true purpose for the tithe for too long. And in the process, we have short-circuited the guaranteed blessings God has said he would provide.

As you read this book ask yourself this question: Am I willing to trust God's wisdom more than my own regarding the tithe? If you can say "Yes" to that question, I pray for you to see with new eyes what God can and will do in your life.

Overseer Victor Scott +
Executive Pastor
Ambassadors of Christ Ministries
May 2020

Introduction

$\mathscr{I}$ have been in church all my life. During all those years, I have

seen and heard every possible argument in favor and against tithing. In my home church, tithing was never an issue. We all understood that Christians tithe. That was it. It was not very complicated—Christians bring the tenth of their earnings to the church to support the ministry, the infrastructure, and the pastor. Most of the churches only had one pastor, therefore, the pastoral support was directed at one person—the local pastor. I don't remember church members complaining about the tithe, or even hearing a lot of teaching regarding this subject. As a child, it just appeared that people knew that tithing was what Christians were supposed to do, even if not everybody gave their tithe. This fact has been the norm in the church for hundreds of years—most people simply do not understand or feel the need to tithe.

Tithing has been debated for years with people coming down on one of two sides. One side holds that tithing is a biblical mandate that applies to Christians today. The other side believes that the tithe is out of date and God's call is for Christians today is to give "as they have purposed in their hearts" (2 Cor. 9:7). Both sides are sincere in their beliefs, and I believe that both are doing the best they can to explain the biblical message regarding giving to support the church's ministries and vocational minister. Churches that rely on the tithe have met their financial obligations for centuries, and churches that rely on regular offerings have also met their obligations.

However, there are two little secrets that I want to point out. On the one hand the churches that depend on the tithe have not been able to convince all their members to tithe faithfully, even though they have been able to survive without a full tithe. On the other hand, the churches that depend of the generous offerings model still use the ten percent (the tithe) to measure whether their members are being truly generous in their giving. Even though this secret is not mentioned out loud , the fact is that nobody believes that giving two percent of their incomes is a strong sign of a generous giver. That is, if people who depended on the generous giving model started receiving an average of one percent of people's incomes, their view of generosity would suffer a dramatic change. The bottom line is that generous Christians always give more than ten percent of their income to the church as an act of obedience to Christ because they believe that God requires the tithe to support his mission on earth. So, if faithful believers on both sides of the debate always give more than the tithe, what is this debate really all about?

Let me share with you that this debate is *not* about making Christians tithe or to make them more generous. My statement may confuse some of the readers but follow me for a minute. According to some statistics only five percent of all Christians in the United States give enough of their incomes to the church to even reach the tithe. Imagine that! Only five percent. We can ask the fair questions: what is the ninety five percent doing? Why is it that only five percent of Christians tithe? But the same question applies to the other side of the debate. Where are all the generous givers? For no one can convince me that five percent giving at least the tithe represents an avalanche of generous giving. The most logical conclusion is that neither the tithers nor the generous givers are doing what they claim they believe.

As the readers can quickly appreciate neither the pro-tithe teachers nor the pro generous giving teachers have convinced their churches to do either. The only thing that is certain is that faithful Christians (the 5%) will always give more than the tithe, and they never complain about giving as much as they do. In reality, about 80% of all Christians only give about 1.2 percent of their income to the church. Forget the tithers. Forget the generous givers. One-point-two percent of people's income is neither a tithe nor generous giving.

The debate about tithing reminds me of the anecdotal question from the Dark Ages in which theologians were debating how many angels can fit on the head of a pin? I believe that in the same way the Dark Ages theologians missed the point, modern day theologians have missed the point about the tithe as well. If the readers are wondering why I can make such an outrageous statement, I will take the rest of this book to explain my perspective, but I hope that by the end of this short book, the readers will know the answer.

Over the next three chapters I will follow a simple outline. In Chapter One I will present a theology and primary purpose of tithing. In Chapter Two I will discuss the covenantal origin of the tithe that makes it an eternal discipline. And in Chapter Three I will answer some of the most common misconceptions about tithing.

I invite the reader to follow along and to make your own mind regarding the tithe. God bless you all.

Chapter One

A Theology of Tithing

Bottom Line Up Front: *The tithe is God's method to measure humanity's level of greed.*

The apostle John related an event in which a woman named Mary approaches Jesus with a very expensive perfume bottle to anoint Jesus (Jn. 12:1-8). Without going into the details of the extraordinary meaning of this event, I want to refer to a phrase that John included in his narrative that sheds light on our discussion. After Mary finished anointing the Lord, John quoted Judas Iscariot as asking: "Why was this perfume not sold for three hundred denarii, and given to the poor?" (Jn. 12:5).

At first glance Judas appeared to be concerned with the needs of the poor, but the apostle John added a clarifying parenthesis about Judas's intentions. Read the apostle's words with me: "But [Judas] said this, not because he cared for the poor, but because he was a thief, and having charge of the moneybag, he used to help himself to what was put into it" (Jn. 12:6).

Judas was the classic prototype of greed. His love of money had led him to steal from the money that Christ received to sustain the ministry all the disciples. As we all know, the love of money not only dragged Judas to steal from the offerings, but later he betrayed the Lord for the miserable sum of thirty pieces of silver. Judas represents the thief who does not understand the dangers of stealing from God and who believes that he can hide his intentions from the Lord's penetrating eyes. Of all the evils that come from greed, possibly betraying the Lord is the greatest.

If the tithe measures whether we have conquered greed, as I argue in this book, then withholding the tithe puts us at risk of betraying the Lord when we replace him as the Giver of life, with Mammon the god money, or of greed.

Christian leaders have debated the issue of tithing for years. Most believe that tithing is the most legitimate way to support the ministries of the Church. There is another group that considers tithing obsolete as being an Old Testament teaching. In this book, I take the position that tithing is a spiritual discipline with a spiritual purpose for believers. Throughout the rest of this book I will defend the spiritual purpose of tithing as an instrument that God uses to remove greed from the hearts of believers.

The Church and Scripture have been clear on the responsibility of the faithful to support the mission of the kingdom of God. In this book I am not going to debate the validity of that proposal. Here I want to introduce the theological principle that tithing goes beyond the practical application of generosity. We don't need a debate about tithing. We need to debate how we can transform believers' hearts to become generous with their finances. In reality we need a debate about the hidden idol in too many of our churches which is the love of money or greed. I will repeat often that before we become generous, we need to break the hold greed has on our spirits, and God designed the tithe for that very purpose.

I think the first issue I need to address is my perspective of tithing as a theological maxim. Once we have a clearer theological understanding of God's purpose for generosity, then, and only then, we will be able to decide how we should proceed in one way or another. I believe God intended to have a spiritual definition and purpose for the tithe. That is, since God does not have any use for material things, such as money, then, his purpose for the tithe must be related to his design to transform the human condition. Let me be blunt. God couldn't care less about our money or our possessions. His focus is on "transforming us into the image of Christ," and, I would imagine that freeing us from idolatry would be an integral part of that purpose. I would add that, as a means to cleanse our hearts from idolatry, God would also want to remove the human craving for money.

By now the readers know that, on this debate, I am on the side of the tithe. I do not teach the tithe at the expense of generous giving, nor do I teach the tithe as a practical or as a financial matter. As a matter of fact, I do not even teach the tithe as a church or religious imperative. I believe the tithe is God's yardstick to measure to what extent Christians have dislodged themselves from the love of money, or greed. Since the love of money is idolatry, it is contrary to God's character and design. Thus, it is imperative for Christians to embark on a journey to die to self and become more like our Savior who was totally dependent of the Father's leading in his life. Jesus, speaking about the dangers of greed, said that, "No one can serve two masters, for either he will hate the one and love the other, or he will be devoted to the one and despise the other. You cannot serve God and money" (Matt. 6:24).

Did you catch the end of the text? Jesus's identified the two masters as God and money. Imagine that! Jesus knew that believers' greatest danger was not replacing the Lord with the worship of Ba'al or Moloch or any other false god. Our greatest challenge is to remove our love of money from our hearts and replace it with our love of God. When we come into the Christian faith, God's image in us has been distorted by sin and it has become selfish and greedy. If we are going to foster a deeper intimacy with the Lord, we must replace these character flaws with God's grace and generosity. As a result of the human predisposition toward greed, Jesus spent a great deal of time correcting people's perceptions about money.

We know Jesus related some thirty-plus parables in the gospels, and of all those parables, more than twenty dealt with money in one form or another. Actually, Jesus spoke about money and hell more than he did about grace and love.

A Word on the Hermeneutical Issue

In my estimation, the two main arguments of this debate make the same hermeneutical mistake. Both sides argue their positions but without including how God's character or how God's attribute of impartiality informs the spiritual nature of the tithe. In other words, the proponents of the tithe do not even ask the question of why a spiritual God, who does not need anything from the physical world, would demand the tithe, besides the obvious need to support the temple in the Old Testament and the church in the New. Similarly, the proponents of generous giving do not ask the question why God expects generosity from his people, besides the concept of reaping a generous harvest.

Another question these writers have never asked is; why did God accuse the people of robbing him by withholding the tithe? Think about this. The people were *robbing* God! This was strong language, but how can a mere mortal rob God of anything? Certainly, the prophet did not imply that people have the power to pry open God's safety box and take his possessions!

I think a few clarifications regarding God's character are in order to set the stage for the rest of this book. I want us to explore together the two critical theological principles that remove the tithe from the financial/physical realm and shifts it to that of being a spiritual discipline to match God's spiritual purposes for humanity. I want to reiterate that I believe the tithe, is primarily a spiritual issue, and we have to discuss it from that perspective.

Let's take a closer look at the two primary theological issues related to the tithe: God's divine prerogative to receive the tithe, and the tithe as God's yardstick to measure human greed. They are both of equal importance because they are both related to God's character.

The Tithe is a Divine Prerogative

I have always found the prophet Malachi's tone in this passage very curious. The Lord accused the people of breaking the covenant. He said: "Ever since the time of your ancestors you have turned away from my decrees and have not kept them. Return to me, and I will return to you" (Mal. 3:7). The context of this chapter is Israel's disobedience that manifested itself through their withholding the tithe.

The Lord continued. "But you ask, 'How are we to return?' "Will a mere mortal rob God? Yet you rob me" (Mal. 3:7b-8a). This is the phrase that has always puzzled me. What did the prophet mean with the statement that the people had robbed God? How can people rob God of anything? What does God have of physical value that people can take from him by force or guile? The prophet's language does not make sense if we he was referring to anything of physical value. Therefore, whatever the people had robbed from God it was not physical.

Nevertheless, when the people protested by asking how they had robbed the Lord, the prophet answered this way: "In the tithes and offerings" (Mal. 3:8). If the people do not have the power to take anything from God, then, the tithes and offering must have represented something spiritual. It is in this phrase that I find the most important theological message from Malachi to the people of Israel, and to us today.

If the Lord does not need anything physical from us, and if there is nothing we can offer the Lord in exchange for our relationship with him, what could this verse possibly mean? That is, God does not have banks to save money or convenience stores to buy groceries. God does not have a safe to hide the money in his house, and yet, the prophet expressed the Lord's displeasure in the strongest possible terms—the people had robbed something of value from the Lord.

The dictionary defines the word robbery as "the felonious taking of the property of another from his or her person or in his or her immediate presence, against his or her will, by violence or intimidation."[1] If we use this definition for robbery, there is no possible way that the people had the means or the power to take anything away from God. Additionally, we would have to agree that since the Lord does not have any physical money, then, when Israel withheld the tithes and offerings they were robbing God of something of spiritual value that belonged to the Lord. We know the Bible has stated that the tithe belongs to the Lord, but we know the reason the tithe belongs to the Lord is **not** its monetary value. Also, I have already mentioned the primary purpose for the tithe, which from this book's perspective seeks to reconcile the people with God.

If the tithe serves as an antidote against idolatry, then, when people keep the tithe for personal uses, they are claiming they are as entitled to the tithe as the Lord. The robbery was not about money per se. The robbery was about what the tithe represented, which was prerogative to be only Lord in people's lives. The people had robbed God of his place as the only Lord of the nation. Please consider the following statement: *When the people kept the tithe for themselves, they willfully appropriated God's exclusive prerogative as the only God of the universe.* In other words, when the people do not give their tithes to the Lord, they are in fact claiming to have the same divine prerogative as the Lord, and they have become idols unto themselves.

The theological issue around God's divine prerogative is not a minor issue. Only the Lord is God and there is not one else like him. The first commandment was very specific on this point. "Thou shall have no other gods before me" (Ex. 20:3). Since the love of money is idolatry, then, by keeping the tithe for personal use, they were replacing

---

[1] Dictionary.com. https://www.dictionary.com/browse/robbery?s=t

the Lord as their only God with greed. Therefore, God's complaint was not about the two goats and one sheep the people owed him. God complained that through withholding the tithe, the people had replaced the Lord with themselves. That was the reason he had asked them to return to him.

Let me expand on the biblical usage of the phrase to rob God. Taylor and Clendenen have stated that "the word used in Malachi 3:8–9 for "rob" (*qāba ʿ*) occurs elsewhere only in Proverbs 22:23, where it is used as a synonym for *gāzal*, which means to take by force, rob, plunder.[2] They added that "as the priests in Malachi 1:6–7 had not considered their carelessness with the sacrifices to be a personal insult to God, so the people here claim unawareness that in withholding from the temple and its priesthood they were robbing God."[3] The term for "man" here is *ʾādām*. The creature dares to rob from the Creator, just like Adam and Eve attempted to take for themselves the title of being gods in the Garden of Eden (Gen 1:27; 2:7; 5:1; 9:6; Duet 4:32).[4]

When we consider how the priests had insulted the Lord with their careless sacrifices, the phrase that the people were robbing God makes more sense. Keeping the tithe for themselves would have been akin to offering sacrifices to themselves. In other words, the problem was not the money. The problem was they had replaced the Lord with themselves. They had become the gods of their lives as a result of their greed, as Adam and Eve attempted to do in the Garden of Eden.

Let me share a passage from a different context that helped me confirm the interpretation I have suggested that by keeping the tithe for themselves, the people in fact had appropriated for themselves a prerogative that belongs to God—which is to be the only Lord in their hearts. This prerogative is the reason the Lord summons the people to return to him.

---

[2] R. A. Taylor, & E. R. Clendenen, (2004). *Haggai, Malachi* (Vol. 21A, p. 418). Nashville: Broadman & Holman Publishers.
[3] Ibid.
[4] Ibid.

In his letter to the Philippians, the apostle Paul made a rather strange statement when speaking about Jesus's humility. His desire was for believers to become humble like Jesus, but in the process, he used a phrase that took me back to Malachi 3. Read it with me.

> [5] In your relationships with one another, have the same mindset as Christ Jesus: [6] *Who, being in very nature God, did not consider equality with God something to be used to his own advantage*; (emphasis added) [7] rather, he made himself nothing by taking the very nature of a servant, being made in human likeness. [8] And being found in appearance as a man, he humbled himself by becoming obedient to death—even death on a cross! (Phil. 2:5-8 NIV).

The ESV has the following rendering of this passage: "who, though he was in the form of God, did not count *equality with God* a thing to be grasped" (Phil. 2:6). And the KJV uses this variation of the passage: "Who, being in the form of God, thought it not *robbery* to be equal with God."

Let me point out that the KJV has the most accurate translation of this passage. The phrases in the ESV "*a thing to be grasped*," and the phrase in the NIV "*something to be used for his advantage*" do not come even close to describing the force of Paul's words in this context.

The Greek word Paul used to describe Jesus's action was *arpagmoc* (αρπαγμος).[5] Joshua Dickey defined this word as "the act of seizing; robbery; a thing seized or to be seized booty; to deem anything a prize; a thing to be seized upon or to be held fast, retained."[6] In other words the correct rendering of this word is robbery, as the KJV translated it. The obvious question is, what does it mean that Jesus did not rob God by making himself equal to God?

We can read Paul's message this way: Jesus did not consider he was robbing God when he made himself equal to God because he was

---

[5] Joshua Dickey. The Complete Koine-English Reference Bible: New Testament, Septuagint and Strong's Concordance (Kindle Locations 426033-426034). . Kindle Edition.

[6] Ibid.

God. When Jesus said that he was equal with God he was not replacing or usurping any of God's divine attributes as the Lord of the universe. If Jesus had been a mere mortal, and if he had claimed that he was equal to God, then, he would have robbed God of his divine prerogative.

I believe both, Malachi and Paul, were making reference to the same theological truth: every time a man (*adam*—the creature) takes for himself a role or a characteristic that belongs to God alone, he is robbing God. This was the problem with the priests in Malachi 1 and with the people withholding the tithe in Malachi 3. The people had taken upon themselves a role or a prerogative that belonged to the Lord. They, therefore, were robbing God.

However, when Jesus made himself equal to God, he did not rob God because *He is equal to God*. People rob God when they assume for themselves a quality of God's character and nature or a prerogative that only belongs to God. The tithe belongs to God, but when the people kept the tithe for themselves, they declared that they had the same right as God to receive the tithe, and thus, they are robbing God of something that rightly belongs to him, which is his Lordship over his creation.

Greed is The Issue

Luke recorded the story of a rich ruler who came to Jesus to inquire about the requirements to inherit eternal life (Lk. 18:18-30). Jesus answered the ruler that he needed to obey the commandments, to which the ruler answered that he had kept all the commandments from his youth. The ruler's answer opened the door for Jesus to challenge the ruler's assumptions about the law, and his presumptions about his own righteousness. But, primarily, Jesus used the ruler's arrogance to force him to look inside himself and confront the one flaw he had never considered about himself: his greed.

If we follow Jesus's statement we will notice that he did not identify the ruler's problem but instead, Jesus issued a challenged that woud reveal the ruler's flaw. Jesus said to him, "sell everything he had and distribute to the poor, and you will have treasure in heaven" (Lk. 18:22). With this statement Jesus let the ruler know that he was not as perfect as he thought, and that his love for, and dependence on, money prevented him from inheriting eternal life. He had placed his love for money above his love for God, and his response to Jesus's challenge exposed the hidden condition of his heart. Read it with me. "But when he heard these things, he became very sad, for he was extremely rich" (Lk. 18:22).

The rich ruler walked away sad because he loved his money more than he loved the possibility of inheriting eternal life. Additionally, the ruler's response to Jesus revealed that adherence to the external requirements of the law was not sufficient to inherit eternal life. After the ruler had left, Jesus made the astounding statement that "it is easier for a camel to go through the eye of a needle than for a rich person to enter the kingdom of heaven" (Lk. 18:25). The eye of a needle, regardless of how it is interpreted, is not big enough for a camel to go through.

I believe we need to make a careful clarification regarding Jesus's words. Since we know that many saints were very rich people, such as Job, Abraham, David, Solomon, and even Lazarus and his sisters in the New Testament, it is not congruent to say that Jesus was, specifically, anti-wealth. Some of the people who supported Jesus were rich, like Joanna, who had supported Jesus from the beginning of his ministry in Galilee. We know Joanna was wealthy because she was married to Chuza, who was king Herod's household manager (Lk. 8:1-3).

Therefore, Jesus was not concerned with the rich ruler's wealth. His concern was about something else, as the context confirmed. When the ruler walked away from Jesus sad, he revealed his heart. He loved his fortune, and money was his god. That Jesus did not care about the ruler's money is clear from the fact that the ruler's response was sadness because he was "extremely rich." We could very easily replace the phrase "extremely rich" with "extremely greedy" without altering the meaning of Jesus's words. Jesus knew this detail about the ruler's heart, and he exposed it for our benefit. Based on the knowledge that the man was bragging about his obedience to the law, Jesus tested the man's heart by asking him to sell everything he had. The rich ruler failed the test when he walked away sad.

The church today is dealing with the same issue as the rich ruler. We have accepted God's gift of eternal life, but we still have not figured out how to get rid of greed. I know some Christians may object to my characterization, but the evidence is that the twenty first century Church, as a whole, only gives 2.5 percent of all its income to God's work. The only people who give less than that to the Church are atheists and the homeless. It is an absolute miracle the Church has survived for two thousand years with so much idolatry within our ranks.

If you notice, Jesus did not accuse the rich ruler of being greedy. However, Jesus used his knowledge of human nature to put the ruler in a position that he had to make a choice. Jesus did this often. In this case, Jesus did not make any accusations or even insinuations of what he believed about the ruler. He simply put him between the rock and the hard place. If he wanted to be perfect, which is God's requirement for heaven, he needed to get rid of his greed. Jesus had put him in an *either-or* situation, and he could not escape. He either sold all his possessions, and conquered greed, or he kept his possessions and forfeited eternal life, which was the reason he came to Jesus in the first place.

While most of us see life in shades of gray, Jesus presented God's kingdom as a day or night option. On one occasion Jesus said, "whoever is not with me, is against me" (Matt. 12:30). In Jesus's world we cannot be in the darkness and in the light at the same time. We cannot be dead and alive at the same time. These dichotomies do not have shades of gray. Thus, Jesus's statement that we cannot serve two masters, means that God is exclusive. God does not take second place, nor does he compete with false gods. In the Lukan passage we can see that the rich ruler understood Jesus's message, but it did not lead the man to repentance. He had been devoted to the law, or so he thought, but he had not been devoted to God. The ruler's worst mistake was to assume that he could sneak into heaven while serving two masters, money and God.

It is important to note that Luke followed the rich ruler's story with another rich man's story that had a different ending. The rich ruler preferred his wealth, while Zacchaeus surrendered his heart to Jesus. Let's look at the contrast.

Generosity is Evidence of Genuine Faith

One chapter after the meeting with the rich ruler, Luke related a different encounter Jesus had with another rich man. This second man did not make any claims of his adherence to the law. He did not have any illusions of righteousness, even though he was also very wealthy. This particular rich man did not have a good reputation within his community, and he was considered an outcast because he had sold his soul to the Romans for money. This man's name was Zacchaeus, and he was a tax collector. The community used the pejorative nickname of a publican. These individuals "collected taxes for the government and were regarded as sinners."[7] Often the New Testament writers used the phrase "tax collectors and sinners" as synonymous (Matt. 19:10-11; Lk. 5:30). Zacchaeus had risen to the rank of "chief tax collector" who had amassed considerable wealth (Lk. 19:2). We need to keep in mind that Luke used the label "chief tax collector" to indicate that Zacchaeus was among the biggest sinners. He was their chief.

Luke identified Zacchaeus as a man of small stature. This phrase also has the symbolic meaning that Zacchaeus was a man of little influence in the community, his wealth notwithstanding (Lk. 19:1-8). On that day, Jesus entered the house of the biggest sinner in Jericho.

If you notice in this story, Jesus did not confront Zacchaeus or challenge him to sell everything he had. Jesus did not even ask

---

[7] Elwell, W. A., & Comfort, P. W. (2001). In *Tyndale Bible dictionary* (p. 1241). Wheaton, IL: Tyndale House Publishers.

Zacchaeus to quit his job. The Lord simply entered Zacchaeus's house and shared a meal with the man of small stature who was the chief of sinners. Luke recorded the reaction of the bystanders thus: "And when they saw it, they grumbled, 'He has gone in to be the guest of a man who is a sinner'" (Lk. 19:7). The crowd knew about Zacchaeus's reputation, and they despised him.

This statement made it unnecessary for Jesus to point out Zacchaeus's sins, or for Zacchaeus to make any specific confession. His sins against the community were well documented. However, after they had concluded the meal, Zacchaeus made an astounding declaration that identified him as someone who had truly believed Jesus's message. Read it with me. "Behold, Lord, the half of my goods I give to the poor. And if I have defrauded anyone of anything, I restore it fourfold" (Lk. 19:8).

It is worth noting that Jesus told the rich ruler to sell everything and give it to the poor, but he did not have the same requirement for Zacchaeus. In Zacchaeus's case, Jesus let him choose how to express his generosity. Zacchaeus offered to give half of his possessions to the poor and apparently, Jesus thought this was a fair offer. As icing on the cake, Zacchaeus went even further and offered to restore fourfold to anyone he had defrauded.

I do not want the reader to miss the following point. To the man consumed with greed, who had a conceited righteousness attitude, Jesus demanded that he sell everything he had and give it to the poor. To the man without any pretentiousness, who was considered the chief of sinners, Jesus did not even challenge his fifty percent offer. In fact, Jesus did not even request Zacchaeus to do anything in particular with his money. Luke did not include Jesus's conversation with Zacchaeus in his narrative, but Zacchaeus generous response was enough evidence that he had accepted Jesus's message. I would venture say that if the rich ruler had come to Jesus with the attitude that he was willing to share his wealth with the poor, Jesus would not have asked him to sell everything he had. Unfortunately, that was not the rich ruler's attitude.

One of the reasons Luke connected these two encounters was, precisely, to make the point that Jesus was not concerned with these men's money. He was concerned with the attitude of their hearts. Generosity is one of the key evidences of true faith in the Bible. The rich ruler did not have it, but Zacchaeus did.

Luke's narratives illustrate the two attitudes people exhibit regarding money. The rich ruler probably worked hard to earn his money, and he felt entitled to keep all of it. He might even have been an honest man in his business. Zacchaeus, on the other hand, used the power of the Roman army to coerce people into paying their taxes, and while all indicators are that he tried to be an honest man, he might have wronged some people along the way, or allowed those he supervised to squeeze more money than it was required from their neighbors. The rich ruler and Zacchaeus were different in another significant way. The ruler believed in his own righteousness, but Zacchaeus did not have any pretensions of being righteous. The rich ruler felt entitled to enter heaven. Zacchaeus did not even think he was worthy to have Jesus enter his house.

The centrality of greed, as a motivator for "all kinds of evil" (1 Tim. 6:10), is the one aspect of tithing that has been ignored by both sides of the argument. I have read several books on tithing and giving, and I have not read one single line dealing with the issue of greed. For our purposes in this book, I have defined greed as an anti-generosity attitude in the human heart. Since authentic faith in God manifests through generosity, then, the need to overcome greed is the reason the biblical writers dedicated so much writing space explaining the nefarious effects greed has on people's relationship with God and with neighbor.

Primary Purpose for the Tithe

In this book I present the new theological principle that the tithe is the yardstick God uses to measure level of greed in the human heart.

I venture say this is a new principle because I have never heard anyone make the argument I am advancing here. If the tithe, from God's perspective, is a spiritual tool that can help us develop a clear picture of where we stand in our love for God, then, the tithe is not a simplistic *quid pro quo* between our giving and God's blessings. Thus, Christians can ascertain their devotion to God through their tithe. When we give less than the ten percent, we know exactly how far we are from overcoming our love of money. Conversely, when we give the tithe or more, we know we have defeated the greed cycle, and we can begin living in spiritual, physical, and financial abundance.

I believe it is crucial to reemphasize that God's creation functions as an agricultural system. When I say that we live in an agricultural system, I mean that everything on this earth is based on the seedtime and harvest principle. From the vegetables we grow, to the attitudes we exhibit in our relationships with people, to our faith in God, all of these, and more, are based on our understanding of seedtime and harvest. The apostle Paul stated this law this way: "Do not be deceived: God is not mocked, for whatever one sows, that will he also reap" (Gal. 6:7).

The world uses a couple of different phrases to describe the seedtime and harvest law. The scientific world uses the phrase "cause and effect," and some eastern religions use the word "karma." A cause and effect relationship can be best described when one action directly results in a specific effect. We can also say that a cause and effect relationship exists when there is a direct link between an action and subsequent reaction to the original action. The cause and effect law is true as it relates to physical chain reactions of events, but this law fails to account for the spiritual or moral nature of actions and effects.

Karma is the second word that can describe the law of the harvest. The Oxford dictionary defines karma as "the sum of a person's actions in this and previous states of existence, viewed as deciding their fate in future existences."[8] The Merriam-Webster dictionary defined karma as "the force generated by a person's actions held in Hinduism and Buddhism to perpetuate transmigration, and in its ethical consequences to determine the nature of the person's next existence."[9] The reader will note that karma describes the eastern religion belief that a person's *future* life, after reincarnation, is determined by the life they are currently living. Many people use the word karma in common conversations to mean that whenever a person does something bad, he will get a consequence for his actions.

For example. Let's say a man robs the neighborhood convenience store, and as he tries to make his escape, his car crashes with a police car and gets caught with the loot from the store. In the common understanding, the thief just experienced karma. But this is not the actual meaning of karma.

The biblical concept of sowing and reaping has always meant that the harvest is greater than the seed. For instance, if I sow one little kernel of corn, I will receive corn as the result, but I will not receive one corn. Instead, I will receive dozens of individual ears of corns attached to the corn plant. In the cause and effect law, we may have a series of events related to the original cause, but the effect must always have a direct correlation to the cause, but it is not always equivalent to the cause.

The Christians law of seed and harvest is also different from karma in that we do not believe in reincarnation. We believe in the resurrection. However, for the Christian the resurrection is not directly connected to how we live on this earth. Instead, the resurrection is a harvest independent of our good or bad works. The resurrection is a harvest of grace, and grace does not depend on the actions of the person who receives it. Grace, as an unmerited favor, belongs entirely to the grace giver. When people accept God's gift of eternal life in the person

---

[8] The Oxford Dictionary. https://www.lexico.com/en/definition/karma
[9] Merriam-Webster Dictionary. https://www.merriam-webster.com/dictionary/karma

of Jesus Christ, they receive the harvest of eternal life without any conditions for the receiver of grace, outside of the willingness to accept the gift.

Therefore, the sowing and reaping law is uniquely Christian in that it includes our daily lives, our emotional relationships with people, the spiritual relationship with God, and with God's moral law. Additionally, the law of sowing and reaping is based on grace. Grace is the reason the harvest is always greater than the seed. If I plant a mango seed, I will not receive one mango in return. On the contrary. I will receive twenty or thirty years of mango harvests with thousands upon thousands of mangoes. Let me share briefly how the law of seedtime and harvest (sowing and reaping) relates to the tithe.

The Tithe And The Law of The Harvest

As I have already stated, the tithe measures the level of greed of the human heart. The Bible defines greed as the love of money or the attitude of the heart that prioritizes money over everything else, including God. The apostle Paul went even further and described covetousness as idolatry (Col. 3:5). The Greek word pleonexia ($\pi\lambda\varepsilon ov\varepsilon\xi\iota\alpha$)[10] translated in Colossians as covetousness is synonymous with a "greedy desire to have more."[11] This greedy desire is addictive. The individuals afflicted by it are willing to do anything to satisfy this craving. Let me share two critical consequences the love of money has on people.

First of all, greed, as a form of idolatry, creates a relational barrier between humanity and God. The love of money means that Mammon (the god of money) is the lord of this person's life replacing the true Lord, Creator of heaven and earth. Whenever we replaced the

---

[10] Dickey, (Kindle Location 440126). . Kindle Edition.
[11] Ibid.

Lord with any idol, we are robbing God of his prerogative as Creator and Sovereign over his creation and creatures. Obviously, when people vow down before false gods, they are functioning against their best interests because false gods cannot answer prayers and cannot bring blessings into people's lives. One of the dilemmas people face every day is their desire to receive God's blessing while at the same time living in rebellion against the Lord. Many people don't even realize that it is not possible to reject the Lord and to expect his blessings at the same time.

When the prophet Malachi called the people to return, he also included what they needed to do in order to restore their fellowship with God. They needed to bring their tithe to the storehouse. Think about this for one moment. Once they have begun bringing the tithe, the Lord would open the windows of heaven, not before. In God's kingdom, the seedtime must always precede the harvest. Always.

The second consequence of greed, as the apostle Paul had said, is that the love of money is the cause of all kinds of evil. This is not a minor point. The evil that follows the love of money is so prevalent that we even have a proverb to identify people's motivation for their evil deeds—"follow the money." If we follow the money, we will find out who and why the evil deed was done. At the end of almost every crime we can find money and power as the driving forces. Thus, God instituted the tithe to measure our level of greed with the express purpose of awakening the human heart to God's grace to facilitate our return to the Lord. His desire was for the people to acknowledge him as the only true God of the universe, and of our lives. I can say, then, that God's purpose was to prevent that the people to engaged in all kinds of evil desires motivated by greed. These evils desires and actions can cause irreparable harm on others and have a detrimental consequence on our relationship with God.

In God's agricultural system, the tithe is the seed, and the reaping includes our reconciliation with God and the blessing to receive the benefits of the secondary results of the tithe. Please remember that

30

abundant living begins after we have broken the wall built by greed that separates us from God. Thus, I support the principle that the tithe is the essential element that transforms our perspective to have a mindset that is more congruent with God's generous character. I can use Jesus's words here. "render to Caesar the things that are Caesar's, and to God the things that are God's" (Lk. 20:25). Caesar's image on the coin, made him the lord of the physical tax. God's image in us makes him the Master of our spiritual lives. Our options are quite simple. We either give to God what belongs to him, which is his image in us, or we can continue believing that Caesar is our master because he controls our finances.

God is Spirit

Since I grew up in church, I have always known that God is Spirit, but as I got older, the phrase took a deeper meaning. I began to realize that as a Spirit, God does not occupy space and he does not exist in time. He exists outside the created order, and he does not need anything from creation. As I continued to develop these concepts, I became more aware that as a Spirit, God must have a spiritual purpose for everything he does or demands of us, including the tithe. That is, if God does not need our money or anything physical to accomplish his purposes, then, the tithe cannot have a physical purpose for God.

Please remember that the tithe's utility only has meaning within creation, and since God exists outside creation, the tithe does not have any utility for God. I propose that the tithe's purpose is to elevate God's image in us above the love of money. God expects that his people function from a perspective of generosity, because he is generous, but if we are still kneeling before Mammon's altar, we cannot reflect God's generosity and grace in our hearts and attitudes toward our neighbor.

For several years I have wrestled with two questions in an effort to ascertain how they connect God's character and the tithe. First, if God does not need the tithe, why did he demand it? Second, what spiritual benefit could the tithe have for people? In my search, one thing became clear to me. Whatever God was demanding of us must have a spiritual value. In other words, while we respond to God's commandment with our tithe, the tithe itself is about an attitude of the heart that reflects how much progress we have made in overcoming our love of money. From God's perspective, the tithe opens a window into the human heart that reveals our level of greed. When Christians give the tenth or more to the church with joy, they have overcome the love of money and are ready to begin living in financial and spiritual abundance. Anything short of the tithe is an indication that greed, or the love of money, is still sitting on the throne of our hearts.

God Doesn't Need Our Money

I have already mentioned the concept that God does not need our money, but I believe it's important to make an obvious, but important observation. I cannot tell you how many times people have asked me that "if God does not need our money to accomplish his purposes, why do we have to give our money to the Church?" The question implies that whatever we have actually belong to us. It also implies that since God does not need our money, the tithe is not a spiritual discipline. Nothing can be further from the truth. If we take the question to its logical conclusion, the question also implies that the Church should not even exist because without the offerings of faithful Christians, the ministry could not go on. I don't want the reader to miss my point here. God commanded the tithe for his Church, not for his benefit, but for ours.

I have discovered many secrets in God's word over the years. One of my most significant discoveries is that God's purposes always have multiple layers. For instance, the Church is the Body of Christ and functions as a witness to God's grace that gave to us eternal life through Jesus Christ. Also, the Church is the place in which the saints gather for fellowship, encouragement, and to be witnesses of God's love to the world. Our love for one another is the external evidence that we are Jesus's disciples (Jn. 13:35).

The Church is also a place of healing and sanctification. The love of money is one of the most damaging spiritual failures for the church today. The Church cannot find spiritual healing and become sanctified as long as we are vowing to Mammon. In the Church today, idolatry has taken the form of greed when God's people refuse to give the tithe to the Lord. It is in the act of overcoming greed with our giving of the tithe and offerings that we can see God's primary purpose for the Church; to be generous in all things (2 Cor. 9:11). But as long as Christians continue to keep the tithe of their increase from the Lord, we are still in bondage to the god of money.

I find that if we remove God's designed means for us to overcome greed then, the tithe becomes a shallow financial transaction that fails to accomplish spiritual God's purpose for the tithe. But for too many years, that's exactly how we have described the tithe; as a superficial financial transaction between God and us (we will discuss this more in detail in the next section). Over the course of my ministry, I have approached the tithe as a necessary sacrifice to carry out God's mission through the Church. While this was a legitimate interpretation with good intentions, I was only partly right because the tithe is more than that. One day, I was reading through the psalms and came across a verse I had read many times before, but on this particular day, it grabbed my attention in a different way.

In Psalm 50, Asaph highlighted God's righteousness, power, and the fact that the Lord owns everything. Reading this Psalm, I became curious about the statement that the Lord owns everything. My question was that if God owns everything, why would he ask us for money? Then, in verse 12, Asaph stated that if God was hungry, he would not tell us. Wait a minute here! If Asaph was right, then, why did God insist that Israel owe him the tithe and offerings for the temple? Even though I had asked the right question, I still could not make the connection between the tithe and God's character. But it was a start.

The realization that God does not need anything from me was an eye opener, but not because I did not know that. I have known this all my life, but it became symbolic of my new-found perception of God's character.

Asaph was giving praises to God when the Lord began to speak. The Lord said to Asaph, "I will not accept a bull from your house or goats from your folds. For every beast of the forest is mine, the cattle on a thousand hills" (Ps. 50:9-11). Then, the Lord continued; "If I were hungry, I would not tell you, for the world and its fullness are mine" (Ps. 50:12). When I read this verse, it hit me. If there is nothing we can offer the Lord, to include animal sacrifices, what is it that he wants from us? A couple verses down, the Lord answered my question. He told the psalmist, "Offer to God a sacrifice of thanksgiving and perform your vows to the Most High" (Ps. 50:14). Since I am a curious person, I had to ask another question. If all God desires from us is a "sacrifice of thanksgiving," why was he so meticulous and demanding regarding animal sacrifices and financial offerings in the Old Testament?

I began to notice the same pattern in other areas of the Bible. For instance, God called Gedeon to go to battle with the Medianites (Judges 7). Gideon promptly assembled an army, but the Lord told him that he had too many people, and he needed to send some home. After Gideon sent many soldiers home, only three hundred were left because God did not want the people to think that they had won the battle. The Lord was going to win the battle, and yet, he wanted Gideon to play a role in the victory. We can see this pattern in many other areas of ministry, but this example should suffice.

Even though God does not need anything from us, he still insists that we play a role in accomplishing his purposes. This is the reason he has always called men and women as his ministers. God's blunt statement in verse 12 that "if [he] was hungry, he would not tell [Asaph]" was the clincher for me. God wanted the psalmist, and us, to be generous but not for God's sake, but for ours. We need to learn that generosity is a divine character quality that reveals God's goodness and grace in a person's heart.

God does not need nor wants our possessions. He wants a grateful and willing heart evidenced by our generosity and ability to forgive others. The human ability to be generous has been distorted by selfish ambition. Whether we understand it or not, greed is caused by our sinful condition. Therefore, God's goal with the tithe is to give us a measurable mechanism by which we can overcome greed and begin to live abundantly, which leads to true generosity. Asaph had to overcome his greed and so do we.

The fact that God is spirit and that he does not need anything from us led me to the key principle regarding the tithe. The tithe has nothing to do with God. Rather, the tithe is a human issue. We are the ones who must overcome greed to free ourselves from the most powerful motivator for evil in the world; the love of money. God created us, and he knew the threshold we needed to cross, and the barrier we needed to breakdown, to free ourselves from idolatry. When God designed man, he knew that Adam and Eve would be susceptible to the temptation to be like God. The serpent tempted the first couple, precisely in that detail, when he suggested to Eve that eating the forbidden fruit would grant them a god-like status to rule over the earth (Genesis 3:5).

Since God is generous by nature, he included a built-in mechanism in our design to measure our level of greed. Let me say it in another way. He knew the process we must go through to become like him in our generosity. We have to overcome greed, and the tithe was God's mechanism to achieve this purpose. Let me add that God did not design us with this mechanism for his benefit because he already knows whether we love money more than we love him. He instituted the tithe as an external requirement to help us overcome the spiritual damage greed produces in us. Therefore, when as Christians we give the tithe with joy this becomes the first indicator that we have overcome the love of money, and we can love God as the only master of our lives. Let us take a deeper look at this principle.

Generosity And Forgiveness

Let me begin this section by stating that the tithe's primary purpose is to give us a method to know where we stand on our greed-o-meter, if you will. A person who gives eight percent of his income for God's work is closer to overcoming his greed than a person who only gives two percent of his income. The tenth is a very simple method to measure greed. Each percentage point lets believers know whether they are making progress to root out money's supremacy over our lives.

For years I have heard hundreds, if not thousands, of messages on giving, tithing, and financial management. Most preachers and teachers fall on one of two camps when it comes to tithing. The first group are the tithers. The tithers believe the Bible teaches that giving the ten percent of our income is God's means to support all the ministries and needs of the church. This group also makes the distinction that, since the tithe began before the Mosaic Law and, as such, it was not abolished when Jesus fulfilled the law.

The second camp are the "cheerful givers," (2 Cor. 9:18). This side of the equation teaches that tithing was an Old Testament practice that only applied to ancient Israel, and it plays no role in the New Testament Church. This position also teaches that the tithe was a form of a tax to support the temple and that it does not have any application for the church because the temple is no longer operative. (I will address some of the objections to the tithe in Chapter 3.)

I believe that both camps present very important elements of the truth, but I also believe that both camps err in a very significant way. Most writers, teachers, and preachers I have heard address the concept of giving have one major flaw. They present the tithe as, what I call, *a financial transaction between God and us*. This financial transaction means that if I give God my tithe and offerings, God is obligated to give me back a truckload of money for my enjoyment. I consider this perspective to be simplistic, and it robs the tithe of its most important purpose, which is to guide us to be more like God in our generosity.

I would suggest to you that both sides of the equation are missing the spiritual meaning of the tithe. The tithe is not a financial exchange. Rather, the tithe is a spiritual discipline to transform the human heart from being selfish and greedy to becoming selfless and generous.

Undoubtedly, there is a reciprocity between our generosity for God's kingdom and the financial blessings God has promised, but this financial reciprocity is a secondary result of giving. These secondary purposes are no different from the promises of blessings that God sends to his people when they live in obedience and gratitude. I teach our leaders that the primary benefit of the reciprocity between our generosity and God's blessings is our reconciliation and restoration to intimacy with God. If we remember, Malachi's message was, precisely, that the people needed to return to the Lord (Mal. 3:7b). Our spiritual mindset changes when we tithe, because with the tithe we become more like God's generous character.

There is no greater evidence of God's generosity than when he sent his Son Jesus as a sin offering for the sins of the world. The Bible has a plethora of passages that encourage God's people to be generous. I believe the biblical call for generosity is directly related to God's character quality of goodness. For instance, we read in Psalm 37:21 that, "the righteous is generous and gives." The psalmist also stated that "it is well with the man who deals generously and lends" (Ps. 112:5). And James mentioned God's generosity in giving wisdom to those who ask him (Jam. 1:5).

Generosity is a divine character quality, but it is not exclusive to God. Since God created us in his image, he shared with us all his personhood qualities, and generosity is one of them. We can be generous like God is, but before we develop a generous spirit, we must overcome the selfishness that manifests itself through the love of money. I believe the tithe plays a central role in this process. People's selfish attitude about money is probably the reason Paul told Timothy that "the love of money is the root of all kinds of evil" (1 Tim. 6:10). Paul's statement was an indictment against greed. If you notice, the apostle did not indict money, but the love of money. His reason was that money is an inanimate object without moral value, but greed is a non-physical motivator with moral value.

The second part of the verse is a tremendous challenge for the Church. Paul described the love of money as a craving. When the apostle used the word craving to describe the love of money, he was comparing greed with an addiction. He also stated that because of this craving, "many have wandered away from the faith and pierced themselves with many pangs" (1 Tim. 6:10b). Just imagine how powerful this craving for money is that it goes so far as to derail many from their spiritual journey.

The Greek word translated as craving is *oregomenoi* (ορεγομενοι) which means "to stretch oneself out to reach for something."[12] These are uncontrollable cravings that make people do anything to get what they want, at all costs. If the craved object appears to be out of their reach, they are willing to take any risks to obtain the forbidden prize. In this effort to reach out for money, the apostle Paul warned that greed, or the craving for money, had pushed many Christians to wander away from the faith, and other Christians had added unnecessary suffering to themselves.

The human experience has shown that people are willing to commit the greatest atrocities imaginable for money. Greed motivates many murders, family violence, divorces, and robberies. Even some church closings are the result of poor financial management, and many times, poor financial management is the result of people craving for money. Many friendships have ended as a result of bad loans or borrowed money. Some pastors and Christian leaders have ended up in jail for embezzling church funds. Additionally, some church leaders have destroyed pastors' lives solely for the purpose to control their salaries and manipulate them into submission to their whims.

---

[12] Dickey, (Kindle Location 410993). Kindle Edition

Money is such a powerful influence in people's lives that Jesus even compared a generous attitude with people's ability to forgive each other's offenses. Think about that for a second. I think Jesus was saying that a generous person has a greater capacity for forgiveness than a greedy person. Greed is self-centered, while generosity, by necessity, focuses on the needs of others. Let's read Jesus's words together.

> "Judge not, and you will not be judged; condemn not, and you will not be condemned; forgive, and you will be forgiven; give, and it will be given to you. Good measure, pressed down, shaken together, running over, will be put into your lap. For with the measure you use it will be measured back to you" (Lk. 6:37-38).

Jesus made several assertions in these verses. "Don't judge." "Do not condemn." In this context, Jesus implied that judging and condemning came from similar attitudes. Then, Jesus made two other, apparently independent statements: "forgive, and you will be forgiven," and then he added, "give, and it will be given to you." Did you notice the contrast Jesus was making? The context indicates that judging and condemning come from the same attitude. By a way of contrast, forgiving and giving are on the opposite side of the equation. Thus, generosity and forgiveness share the same motivational source because a person cannot forgive without being generous and vice versa. We must remember that forgiveness is an act of grace, and grace is the giving of an unmerited favor to an unworthy recipient. Or said differently, the lover of money is a judgmental person who has a hard time forgiving others.

I believe that since these verses appear within the same context, it is very possible that Jesus was speaking about the attitude that drove those actions. I would venture say that people with judgmental and condemning attitudes have difficulties forgiving others and has difficulties developing the discipline of giving. Jesus closed this section by saying that those who give generously will receive an abundance of blessings because "with the measure you use it will be measured back to you" (Luke 6:38b).

This last phrase is true of both attitudes. The judgmental person will experience condemnation. The generous person will experience forgiveness. Thus, I propose that the tithe disciplines the believer to be generous and to forgive. We cannot be generous until we break the cycle of greed by bursting beyond the tithe.

The Lukan context points to Jesus connecting forgiveness and generosity. These character qualities proceed from the same attitude of the heart. The person who is not generous will have difficulties with forgiveness. Similarly, the greedy person has the tendency to be judgmental and condemning of others. I believe Jesus connected these two concepts, precisely, because the generous person is a forgiving person, and the greedy person is a judgmental person. I think we can evaluate a person's ability to forgive others based on their generosity. While I don't know who is holding grudges, I know that a generous person is more likely to forgive an offense than the person who is a lover of money.

God knew from the beginning of time that money had the possibility of corrupting the soul, and he gave us the tithe as the formula to correct the corrupting power of greed. Please remember that money is not the issue. The problem is greed, or the love of money, and not money itself. People who want to be free from spiritual blindness caused by their craving for money need to know three fundamental truths.

First, the love of money (or greed) is the root of all kinds of evils (1 Tim. 6:10). Greed has a spiritually blinding effect on people. Solomon stated that "the fear of the Lord is the beginning of wisdom" (Prov. 9:10). If greed is idolatry, and if the beginning of wisdom is the fear of the Lord, then it follows, that greed is a barrier for people's ability to discern spiritual truths. As a result of this break down of wisdom, the person who craves money is willing to do all kinds of evil in order to obtain it, as Paul advised Timothy to protect himself against.

Second, the love of money (greed) turns people into idolaters that have replaced the worship of the Creator with devotion to money. Basically, idolatry means that the individual has enthroned a false god in the place the one true God. I know that most Christians do not replace God intentionally. But, sometimes Christians have the same attitude about money that the rich ruler had. Some Christians deceive themselves that we are keeping Jesus's commandments while being unwilling to sell everything we have and give it to the poor. However, if we had overcome greed, there would be no need to sell everything we own because we would already be living in generosity and spiritual abundance. Unfortunately, the problem is that many Christians still love their money more than they love God, even if they are not aware of it.

Not only that, but the love of money influences how people relate to God. The craving for money sets a false choice between two masters, God and riches. Idolatry was the primary sin in the Old Testament, and it still is the primary sin in the church today. Idolatry in the Old Testament was the worship of the false gods of Israel's neighbors, but the love of money as the New Testament idol.

Third, the love of money (greed) produces a spiritual blindness that prevents people from seeing God's truths. The love of money also prevents us from seeing the wickedness of others, especially those who rule over us. The prophet Malachi used the phrase the "windows of heaven" as a reference to receiving wisdom to manage our finances. This phrase appeared within the context of God calling the people to stop robbing him. The windows of heaven are a metaphor to explain how God opens the spiritual world to our understanding. The prophet's message was that when we give our tithe and offerings we become wiser to make better financial decisions. Thus, giving the tithe is an antidote against the corrupting effects the love of money (greed) has on the soul.

Additional Benefits of The Tithe

For generations, Christians have focused on the secondary results of giving and have ignored the most significant aspects for which the Bible gives so many instructions about financial management, generosity, and giving (tithing). We already saw the primary purpose for the tithe, and now I want to explore a few secondary benefits of it.

I think it's important to share the classic passage about the tithe before continuing with this discussion because the prophet Malachi included the secondary blessings in his prophetical message of repentance. The prophet Malachi wrote,

> Will man rob God? Yet you are robbing me. But you say, 'How have we robbed you?' In your tithes and contributions. You are cursed with a curse, for you are robbing me, the whole nation of you. Bring the full tithe into the storehouse, that there may be food in my house. And thereby put me to the test, says the Lord of hosts, if I will not open the windows of heaven for you and pour down for you a blessing until there is no more need. I will rebuke the devourer for you, so that it will not destroy the fruits of your soil, and your vine in the field shall not fail to bear, says the Lord of hosts. Then all nations will call you blessed, for you will be a land of delight, says the Lord of hosts (Malachi 3:8-12).

This passage presents the clearest description of the tithe, but the prophet presented it within the context of the people "turning aside God's statutes." The people had ignored God's commandments, and in this passage, God challenged them to return to him by stopping "robbing" of what rightly belonged to God. Malachi made a direct connection between the people rejecting the Lord and their robbing him. The most sensible reading of this passage is that the people had become enamored with their financial success, and they had replaced the Lord with Mammon, the god associate with money.

I will deal more directly with the objection that the tithe is an Old Testament obligation in Chapter Three. Suffice it here to say that if a principle has eternal value, it does not matter if it's found in the Old or

New Testament. Since I believe the tithe has eternal value as the measurement of human greed, therefore, it transcends time and its importance did not end when the Old Testament law became obsolete.

The biblical pattern is that whatever God revealed in the Old Testament regarding his character and personhood attributes is also valid in the New Testament. For example: the Hebrew people walked in the desert for forty years before entering the promised land. It's common knowledge that the trip from the Red Sea to Canaan would have only taken them about eleven days. The Bible also tells us that the historical reason the Hebrews spent forty years in the desert was that the spies were afraid of the "men of great height" in the land (Numbers 13:32). But the theological reason the people of Israel could not enter the Promised Land was that their fear of giants was directly related to their slave mentality.

God declared that the entire generation that left Egypt over the age of twenty had to die in the desert to eradicate the slavery mindset they had acquired after four hundred years of captivity in Egypt. As a practical matter, as long as the Church has a slave mentality, we cannot succeed in the Promised Land. The people of Israel expressed their slave mentality with phrases like, "Would that we had died by the hand of the Lord in the land of Egypt, when we sat by the meat pots and ate bread to the full, for you have brought us out into this wilderness to kill this whole assembly with hunger" (Ex. 16:3). Imagine their attitude. The people with an enslaved mind preferred to trade their new-found freedom, that allowed them freedom to determine their own destinies, for a few crumbs of bread and onions in the land of slavery.

The desert story was about God's redemptive action for Israel and his fulfillment of his promises to Abraham. But the practical application of this events reaches beyond the story itself, and this is what I mean by patterns that have application beyond the initial stories.

The prophet Malachi made one appeal to repentance, one promise of blessing and three secondary blessings. The call to repentance was for the people to stop robbing God and to "bring the full tithe into the storehouse, that there may be food in my house" (Mal. 3:9). Upon repenting, the Lord promised to "open the windows of heaven for you and pour down for you a blessing until there is no more need" (Mal. 3:10). God's promise was so certain that he even challenged the people to test him on his generosity in response to the tithe. If the people repented and responded in obedience with the tithe, God's blessings would overflow the land. Let's take a look at the three secondary blessings associated with the tithe.

First: The Tithe Makes Us Wiser

After the prophet Malachi had pleaded with the people to return back to God, he stated that when the people start tithing again, the Lord will "open the windows of heaven." In other words, tithing breaks the spiritual blindness created by the cycle of greed and makes us wiser regarding God's purpose to bless those who place him at the center of their devotion. Allow me to share two nefarious effects greed has on the mind.

First, greed produces a self-centered and self-absorbed attitude that prevents people from practicing generosity with their neighbors. This selfishness has a blinding effect on people's consciences with the lasting negative result that the person loses the opportunity of celebrating their lives with others or celebrating others' life triumphs.

Second, greed prevents people from grasping the fundamental spiritual nature of the law of sowing and reaping. This law is more than just a reciprocal relationship between a physical seed its corresponding physical harvest. In God's world, spiritual seeds are more important than physical ones. While the law of sowing and reaping works in the physical world, this law is also a metaphor that points to God's world.

Once again, God opens the windows of heaven when people understand that material things are transient and that only eternal things have lasting value. In God's kingdom, people cannot begin to value eternal things until they have broken the cycle of dependence on material things. Or said in another way, until the greed cycle has been broken, we cannot comprehend the spiritual value of our relationship with God, and our hope of eternal life.

Second: The Tithe Protects Our Harvest

When the people give the tithe, the Lord will protect the harvest of the nation. Not only was God going to bless the people beyond what they could comprehend, he was also going to ensure these blessings by protecting the harvest. Malachi said that God "will rebuke the devourer." According to D. J. Clark, "the devourer probably refers to locusts, which traveled in huge swarms and devastated crops."[13] The prophet understood that the word fruit was in reference to all types of crops, and he intended to say that God's protection included all their crops. God promised that if the people would honor him with their tithe, he would protect the land and their harvests.

The tithe as a spiritual principle also has a physical application. Our ability to overcome greed would be an indicator that we have come closer to God's character. As such, God is *faithful* to honor his promises of blessing when we come closer to him. When God promised that he would rebuke the devourer, he was promising that he would protect the physical blessings that would naturally follow the spiritual victory over greed. In addition to protecting the crops from the locust, the Lord would keep the land fertile. The prophet said: "Your field will not be sterile" (Mal. 3:11).

Third: The Tithe Brings Praises to the Lord

The prophet Malachi stated that God's blessings will make Israel a desirable people. The prophet stated that "all nations will call you blessed, for you will be a land of delight" (Mal. 3:12). When we give

---

[13] D. J. Clark, & Hatton, H. A. (2002). *A handbook on Malachi* (p. 447). New York: United Bible Societies.

God what is rightfully his, there will be the extra benefit that our neighbors will see God's blessing in our lives and glorify him.

The tithe does not only evaluate our level of greed. It also allows God to trust us with the finances of the kingdom. Think about that for a second. I have said to people on many occasions that until God can trust us with our own money, he cannot give us the privilege of administering other people's money. This is an important principle. God can only trust us with other people's blessings, if we have already demonstrated that we have overcome greed, and that we are not going to hoard money simply to satisfy our pleasures.

When God's people use their wealth to bless others and advance God's kingdom, God will protect our homes, investments, children, and our wealth. Not only that, but God will increase our blessings so that the world would know that he takes care of those who are faithful to him.

Most of you remember the story of a man who had a great harvest, and he said to himself that he did not even know what to do with his riches (Lk. 12:13-21). Jesus described the attitude of the rich fool with these words: "I will say to my soul, 'Soul, you have ample goods laid up for many years; relax, eat, drink, be merry'" (Lk. 12:19). With this statement we can identify at least two attitudes the man had. First, he did not give thanks to God for his great harvest. He did not even acknowledge that he was *lucky* with his harvest.

The second attitude was his greed. The rich fool said to himself that he was going to enjoy his life, and that he would not even consider anyone else. In the parable Jesus said that the man was going to lose his life that same night. His point was that greedy people do not honor the Lord with their possessions because they are entirely focused in satisfying their selfish desires. Generous people, on the other hand, glorify the Lord with their wealth, and as a result, they also receive the blessings the Lord has promised.

The Roman 13 Confusion

My son Victor sent me a video of Bishop Thomas Henry of Atlanta in which Bishop Henry made a presentation of chapter 13 of the book of Romans.[14] Because of that presentation, I was reminded of some conversations I had c. 1989, during one of my theological seminary courses. Our professor was a strong advocate of liberation theology and was a very intelligent and reasonable educator. On this particular day he gave us the assignment to compare the vision the apostle Paul had presented of the Roman Empire in Romans 13, with the vision the apostle John presented about the same Roman Empire in Revelation 13.

My seminary professor was not convinced the apostle Paul was making a defense of the Roman Empire that extended to all the secular governments in the world. Our professor did not go into detail so that the students would have the debate without being influenced by the professor's opinions. The professor shared two questions that we had to consider in our study. First of all, why was Paul's vision of the Roman Empire so radically different from John's vision? Second, why would Paul have such a benevolent view of the Roman Empire during a time when the Empire crucified Christians, threw them into the arenas to be eaten by lions, or forced them to fight like gladiators?

After leaving the classroom that day, one of my classmates asked what I thought the professor was looking for, especially since we knew his clear adherence to liberation theology? What could you be looking for in a secular government discussion? I told my classmate that I suspected the professor was looking for a way to claim that the United States was not a benevolent country and that using Romans 13 to support the government was wrong. The reader must understand that in the 1980s, according to the rest of the world, the United States represented all the capitalist ills in the world. I did not make a detailed study at the time, but even with my limited knowledge of the passage,

---

[14] Thomas Henry, Jr. Video Message from April 16, 2020.

I came to three conclusions regarding Romans 13 that were reawakened by Bishop Henry's presentation. Let me refer to them to help the reader continue my discussion, as this passage relates to tithing.

My first discovery was the most obvious. The NIV version of the Bible, which was the Bible he was using at the time, adds the word "governing" in Romans 13:1, for the purpose of clarifying the context. I am sure the translators had good intentions, but the word "governing" implies that the apostle Paul was speaking of a secular form of government. However, adding that word is highly questionable, because the word "governing," most likely brought more confusion to the reader, as we will see later.

The real problem with adding this word is that it does not appear in the original Greek version of the passage. The Greek literally says: "All souls to the authorities before him, be subject."[15] Let me rearrange the literal translation so that it makes more sense in English without adding any other words to clarify. The most natural representation, using the most contemporary English grammar would read: "All souls are subject to the authorities over them."

As I listened to Bishop Henry, I realized that the word authority in this context is not primarily a reference to secular governments, but rather, it is a reference to church leadership. Since my seminary years I had doubted that the word authority was a reference to secular governments because I do not believe that Paul was giving authority to the Roman Empire over the life of the Church. I have always said, as an example, that the apostle Paul could not be saying that the Christian church is obliged to submit to the authorities of the atheistic government of Cuba without selling its faith. Therefore, the passage cannot be a general reference to all secular governments around the world.

My second discovery, as I recall, was that it was strange that Paul asked the church located in Rome to submit to the evil Roman Empire

---

[15] Dickey, (Ubicaciones Kindle 398677-398680). . Edición Kindle.

48

that was persecuting them to exterminate them. There is no reference, anywhere in Paul's letters, to suggest that the apostle had such a benevolent vision of Rome. The opposite seems to be true. The apostle challenged the church in Rome to submit to the ecclesiastical ruling authorities, and not to submit to the pagan authorities of the Roman Empire.

My third observation was that the text described the pagan rulers of the Roman Empire as "servants of God," if the most common interpretation is correct. Needless to say, the description that pagan rulers were servants of God seemed a little strange to me. Certainly, the apostle could not be using that description in the sense of his Christian practice. But, I must confess that beyond those observations, I did not dedicate more time to it in the text, until Victor shared with me the message from Bishop Henry. Bishop Henry reminded me of something else. Romans 13 cannot be a call from the apostle for the Church to submit to the authority of secular governments, as we discussed during our class in 1989, but this chapter is a reference to discipline and order in the Church.

In addition to his discussion that the apostle was speaking of church discipline in Romans 13, Bishop Henry added a few words about tithing, which is the subject of this book. Initially, I was not sure how he was tying these issues, but his presentation was solid in both theology and hermeneutics. His discussion prompted me to do some research on my own to confirm his interpretation. Although an exhaustive exegetical study of the entire passage is beyond the scope of this book, I will still refer to various aspects of the passage that confirm Bishop Henry's interpretation of tithing.

If we accept the premise that Romans 13 is in reference to discipline within the church, and not a Pauline endorsement of the Caesars, then our discussion on tithing will make more sense. Based on my personal experience and seminary studies, I will approach this passage from the perspective that the apostle was not endorsing the Roman tyrannical government but was leaving instructions on how the church should relate to the leaders the Lord had established to supervise her.

The NIV version, and several other modern translations, translated the word *phoros* as taxes. The King James Version (1960) uses the literal translation of the word as "tribute". Dickey defined the word tribute (*phoros*) as "a burden, an obligation, or a tax."[16] Bishop Henry suggested that since Romans 13 is about church discipline, then, tribute is the most accurate translation of the word *phoros*, and in this case it should be in reference to tithing because the church does not collect taxes for the government. Once we understand that the apostle Paul was referring to church discipline, we understand that he could not be regulating how the church should pay taxes to secular governments. I think Bishop Henry is right, although this perspective is not the most traditional.

I surveyed seven biblical commentaries to compare their interpretations of this passage and found that all seven assumed that Paul was speaking about secular governments and how the church should submit to these entities because they were "instituted by God." All comments interpreted the passage from that perspective. Boa and Kruidemier shed some light on the subject by suggesting that Paul was using the Levitical system as his historical background.

> The shadows of the Levitical legislation are evident in Paul's next words. Just as the Levites in Israel were supported by the twelve tribes, so the ruling authorities must be supported by taxes on the people.[17]

Boa and Kruidemier correctly assumed that Paul had the Levitical system in mind, but then interpreted the passage as a reference to secular government, a tangent, I believe, is not supported by the text. If it is true that Paul had the Levitical system in mind, it would make more sense for him to have the church in mind, and not the Roman

---

[16] Dickey, (Kindle Location 398677-398680). . Edición Kindle.
[17] Boa, K., & Kruidenier, W. (2000). *Romanos* (Vol. 6, p. 397). Nashville, TN: Broadman & Holman Publishers.

Empire. We must remember the purpose of the Levitical system was to support the temple, and not the government of Israel. The kings ruled Israel, and imposed taxes that went above and beyond the temple tithe. Therefore, in Israel the tithe was separate from the taxes the government demanded. For this reason it would make more sense that, in this passage, Paul was thinking about the church, and not of the Roman Empire.

It would also seem more consistent if Romans 13 were a reference to the church, if Paul had the Levitical system in mind when he used the word "authority" and "servants of God" (*diakonos*). As a result of the connection to the Levitical system, it is less likely that Paul was writing about the submission of the church to a secular and pagan government. Let me make another clarification that supports Bishop Henry's conclusion. The apostle Paul used two different words to refer to the "servants" in this passage. Those words are *diakonos* (deacon) and *leitourgos* (from liturgy).[18] There is something peculiar in these two words. Let's take a look.

The word *leitourgos* appears five times in the New Testament. Paul used it three times, and the writer of Hebrews used it twice. The Bible never used this word in reference to secular rulers or leaders. Dickey's Greek Interlinear Dictionary defined the word *leitourgos* as "a temple or gospel official, or a worshiper of God."[19] I seriously doubt that Paul used a word that means "a worshiper of God" in reference to the Roman rulers and emperors, who were pagans.

The other word that the apostle used in reference to the authorities was *diakonos*. The normal use of *diakonos* in the New Testament refers to "Christian teachers and pastors."[20] Again, it would be extremely strange for Paul to use two words that clearly refer to pastors and other Christian leaders in reference to secular and pagan government officials. In addition to how strange it would have been for

---

[18] Boa, K., & Kruidenier, p. 397
[19] Dickey, (Ubicación Kindle 435825).
[20] Ibid.

Paul to use *diakonos* in reference to pagan leaders, the apostle never used this word in reference to any kind of leadership outside the church. The obvious conclusion is that the apostle would not use these two words, in this specific context, as a reference to leaders outside the church.

For the reasons stated above, I agree that Bishop Henry has the correct interpretation of this passage. The word tribute as a reference to the tithe, then, is the correct reading of the word in question, as opposed to a government tax. Thus, the context requires that we interpret this passage as a reference to Christians who contribute to the Church, not to secular government. In my opinion, then, the apostle Paul was instructing the Church on the need to pay their financial obligation to the authorities over them, who are their bishops, elders, and pastors.

If we accept this interpretation, this would mean that in Romans 13, Paul encouraged the Church to support those who have authority over them with their tribute, which would be synonymous with their tithes and offerings, as was true in the Levitical system. I conclude by saying that, in addition of being the method God uses to measure our level of greed, tithing is also an obligation that Christians have to support the ministries and leaders of the Church. When Christians do not support the Church, everyone suffers and loses the secondary blessings associated with tithing, as God has promised. Tithing reveals how well we reflect God's generous character, and also exposes the idol that has plagued the church for over 2,000 years: greed.

Last Word on The Theological Issue

Let me add three principles that can help us make progress in growing the kingdom of God: (1) we need to know how the world created by God works, (2) God's impartial character does not allow him to change the rules for individuals without a specific plan to advance his kingdom purpose, and (3) our perceptions can change, but our position in God remains the same because God does not change. These three principles determine how God responds to human behavior. Someone may consider himself the smartest person in the world, but if God does not open the windows of heaven and they don't have a personal relationship with him, they will have to depend a human wisdom that is ingrained in a deceptive sinful condition. Additionally, we already know that human wisdom is madness (1 Cor. 2:14).

I think the reason many churches are suffering financially is directly related to Christians inability to conquer greed. In order to conquer greed, we have to experience the spiritual transformation Paul talked about in Romans 12:2. He told the Roman church to "be transformed by the renewing of their minds." We know that a renewed mind leads to transformation. However, most people do not know how to renew their minds. I will share a secret with you that I discovered several years ago: the mind is renewed when we accept the truth of the gospel that replaces the lies we have believed about the world, about ourselves, and about God.

I shared with you the truth that the tithe is God's yardstick to measure human level of greed. This truth places tithing and giving into the realm of a transformed heart that has replaced Mammon, the god of money with the Lord, the God of generosity.

I may have arrived two thousand years too late to the tithing party, but I believe we still have time to reverse the nefarious consequences of greed. We can still transform the rest of history while waiting for Jesus's return. I believe the concept of the tithe as the measurement of human greed is revolutionary, and if churches adopt it and teach it to their congregations, it could transform their members spiritual lives and open the windows of heaven in ways they had never imagined possible.

Chapter Two

Understanding the origin of tithing

Bottom Line Upfront: *Generosity is the natural outcome of overcoming the love of money, not a precursor to it.*

ow that I have made the argument that the tithe is a theological concept that God uses to measure humanity's level of greed, I want to address the origin of the tithe. I will discuss the pertinent passages that give us the background for the tithe. I also want to interpret those passages from a theological perspective, as opposed to a financial one. The church has discussed tithing from a financial paradigm for too long, and those arguments are well known. Thus, I will not rehash those arguments here.

The tithe made its first appearance in Genesis 14:17-20. The scripture relates an encounter between the patriarch Abraham and a mysterious figure named Melchizedek, who was both the high priest of the Most High God and king of the city of Salem. The story does not tell us if Abraham had met Melchizedek prior to this meeting, but they must have met at some point before this encounter because the high priest came to meet the patriarch on his return from battle. That meeting would not have made sense if these two men had never met before. However, if they had met before, then, it makes sense for Melchizedek to have brought a special lunch to share with a victorious Abraham. The encounter between these two men has tremendous theological significance. Melchizedek was a type of Christ, and Abraham received God's covenant regarding the coming of the Messiah and the salvation he would provide for all nations.

This historical figure had received his priesthood from an oath by the Lord himself (Heb. 7:20-22). Since God established Melchizedek's priesthood before the Mosaic Law, his line superseded and outlived Aaron's priesthood, which began with the Mosaic law and ended with Jesus's death. The writer of the book of Hebrews stated that Jesus's priesthood comes from Melchizedek and not from the law, indicating that it was superior to Aaron's priesthood. Let's read the passage and take a closer look at the theological significance of this encounter.

> [17] After his return from the defeat of Chedorlaomer and the kings who were with him, the king of Sodom went out to meet him at the Valley of Shaveh (that is, the King's Valley). [18] And Melchizedek king of Salem brought out bread and wine. (He was priest of God Most High.) [19] And he blessed him and said, "Blessed be Abram by God Most High, Possessor of heaven and earth; [20] and blessed be God Most High, who has delivered your enemies into your hand!" And Abram gave him a tenth of everything (Gen. 14:17-20).

Before I engage the text, I need to add a hermeneutical clarification. I have always shared with my church members, and those who are willing to listen, that we have to always read the Bible from at least two different perspectives. While a particular passage may have more than two levels of interpretation, I am sure every passage has, at the very minimum, two different such levels. I hold this position because I believe the Bible is, at the same time, the revelation of God's character and the revelation of the human condition. Therefore, every passage reveals one or both of these two realities at the same time. We also have to understand the Bible as a book inspired by God to reveal spiritual truths that are not available in the natural order, and they cannot be discerned without God's revealing them to us.

It is important to note that God uses physical elements and historical events to reveal his character. These elements are the instrumental means but not the revelation themselves. I must add that the historical events without the revelation of the spiritual and moral components of God's character are nothing more than stories that people recount. But when we add the revelation of God's character, the events move from being just an assorted series of moments in time and become the specific revelation of God's purposes across time.

If we do not understand these concepts, I think we will lose a large part of God's message in the Scriptures. It is necessary to recognize that when we read the Bible we are dealing with the eternal revelation of the spiritual and eternal nature of God through physical elements and events that people can understand. Therefore, I believe that when God reveals his character through a story or event, he is not inspiring a particular story simply for the benefit of obtaining new information.

Another truth that should be obvious but perhaps overlooked is that we must be able to discern the difference between eternal truths based on the revelation of God's character and, what I call, temporally applied truths revealed for a short period of time to achieve a particular and temporary purpose. I want to clarify that the phrase temporal truth is not a reference to the postmodern philosophy that truth does not exist because it is relative. The phrase truth with temporal application is a reference to a reality that served to condition the behavior or guide a social group for a specific period of time. A more precise definition is that a temporally applicable truth is a situational reality that guides a particular event, and as long as that truth is in force, the people involved will be judged on that truth for a specified period of time. Let me share two examples of truths with temporary application in both testaments by way of illustration. I'm also going to use another more specific Old Testament example related to the law. Let's see.

For example: when God commanded Noah to build the ark because a flood would come, that was a truth with temporary application. Noah built the ark and the flood came, but once that event was consummated, God did not demand that believers continue building arks to this day. At the time of the revelation, the command to build the ark was an absolute truth for Noah and his family, but the command was for a temporary duration. Therefore, although that truth still has spiritual application, it is not an eternal truth that requires that all Christians continue building arks.

Another example of a temporary application truth in the New Testament was the early church practice of having all things in common (Acts 2:44). This truth was so specific, during that short period of time in church history, that Ananias and Sapphira lost their lives to the consequences of that truth. It was true that the main reason for their death was that they lied, but their lie occurred in the context of the reality that the disciples had all things in common. That reality had application at a particular moment in church history, but its intention was not to be prescriptive for the whole Church at all times.

One of the most easily recognizable examples of a truth of temporal application, which is at the same time the most difficult to interpret, is the importance and application of the Mosaic Law. During the time it was in force, beginning at Sinai after the exodus and culminating with the cross of Christ, the Mosaic law governed the religious and political life of the people of Israel. After Jesus died on the cross, and fulfilled the requirements of the law, the Mosaic Law became inoperative and lost its legal and religious power. However, within the period that the law was in force, God revealed many aspects of his character that are still operative today.

Without going into too much detail I will briefly narrate the purposes of the Mosaic Law. One of the purposes of the law was that it codified the sinful condition of human beings by writing the commandments from a negative perspective. The commandment "Thou shalt not kill" was necessary to control the fact that people continued to kill one another, and this was necessary to bring a semblance of social order into Israel. Although God does not yet want us to continue killing other people, the commandment now is "love your neighbor as yourself." In other words, the motivation to respect the sanctity of other people's lives now comes from the image of God in us and not from an external commandment that does not transform the heart.

Moses's encounter with God at Sinai began the dispensation of the law, and the death of Christ on the cross closed the book of Moses in regard to the application of the law to believers. However, all the revelation of God's character and attributes during the period of the law are still effective because God does not change in his person or in his essence.

On the other hand, when I refer to eternal truths, I am speaking of the principles that reveal elements of God's character and attributes. These principles are not limited by time or historical background, and God can reveal them in any situation. For example, when God told Moses to return to Egypt to free his brothers and sisters from Pharaoh's yoke, this was a mandate with temporary functionality and need. However, when the Lord said to Moses, in the same context that his name is "I am what I am," this was a truth with eternal value that transcended Moses's assignment to go to Egypt to free the Hebrew slaves. If we cannot make these distinctions, we will have problems with our hermeneutics, and our understanding of God's revelation will be truncated and deficient.

As I mentioned earlier, the Genesis passage that describes Abraham's encounter with Melchizedek, the high priest of the Most High God, occurred in the context of God establishing an everlasting covenant with Abraham. Melchizedek was the king of Salem and his title literally meant that he was the "king of peace" (Heb. 7:2). The title of "king of peace" lets us know immediately that we are dealing with a character who is a type of Christ. We know that the prophet Isaiah referred to Jesus, the promised Messiah, as the "prince of peace" (Is. 9:

7). This relationship has led many scholars to conclude that Melchizedek was actually what we call a theophany that describes a manifestation of Jesus before his incarnation.

Jesus appeared in the Old Testament on many occasions as the "angel of the Lord." The "angel of the Lord" appeared to Hagar to comfort her after Abraham dismissed her from his house (Gen. 16: 9). He also appeared to Abraham to prevent the patriarch from sacrificing Isaac, who was the son of promise (Gen. 22:11). The "angel of Lord" also appeared to Moses in the midst of the burning bush that was not consumed (Ex. 3: 2). References are too many to list here, but these are sufficient by way of illustration.

While there is a clear connection between Melchizedek and Jesus, most scholars agree that he was a historical figure, "probably a Canaanite prince who retained true faith in the midst of the gloom of surrounding paganism."[21] Regardless of how a person interprets Melchizedek's life, one thing is certain: He was the forerunner of the priesthood of Christ who is independent of the Mosaic Law, and cannot be tied or connected to Moses in any sense of the word. Distinguishing between the two priesthoods is significant because Melchizedek's priesthood was eternal, while Aaron's had temporary application. Similar to Abraham, Melchizedek was a covenant figure who had greater authority than Abraham himself, because he blessed the patriarch, and Abraham gave tithes to Melchizedek (Heb. 7:4).

After Abraham had defeated several kings in battle and had taken the spoils of war, he met Melchizedek on the outskirts of Salem. During their meeting, Abraham recognized that Melchizedek was the high priest of the Most High God and gave him the appropriate tribute that a high priest was entitled to as God's representative. I suggest that tithing has eternal value for two additional reasons; (1) it arose before

---

[21] H. D. M. Spence-Jones, (Ed.). (1909). *Génesis* (p. 209). Londres; Nueva York: Funk & Wagnalls Company.

the law, and (2) it was an exchange between the two main figures that establish the foundation of the Abrahamic covenant.

I want to highlight two elements in Abraham's meeting with Melchizedek that transcend their encounter. These two elements are unique to history, and I believe they were revealed due to their theological significance beyond the event itself. These elements served as a means of grounding what God was revealing about realities that were still hidden in the future.

First, Melchizedek went out to meet Abraham and brought "bread and wine" to share with the patriarch. Despite the fact that bread and wine were commonly used in Israel's ceremonial rituals, and Jesus used these elements to institute the Lord's Supper, most scholars see no theological significance of Melchizedek bringing "bread and wine" to share with Abraham. However, since I believe the Bible is the revelation of God's character and purpose, and since I also believe that Melchizedek is a type of Christ, then, it is not an exaggeration to say that God used this meeting to present the "bread and the wine" as a prophetic utterance that pointed to Jesus. We must remember that Melchizedek presented these two elements more than five hundred years before Moses received the law and before Israel became a nation. It is probable that these elements took off as a consequence of the encounter between Melchizedek and Abraham.

Moses made the connection between Melchizedek's action of bringing "bread and wine" with the fact that he was "priest of the God Most High" (Gen. 14:18). Clearly, in Moses's mind, the fact that Melchizedek brought "bread and wine" to share with Abraham was related to the fact that he was "priest of God Most High." Otherwise, there is no historical reason to insert the parentheses in the statement. He could have just said that he brought bread and wine for dinner. But Moses went further. Moses made a direct connection to the fact that Melchizedek brought "bread and wine" with his role as a priest of the one true God.

Since Jesus was a priest in the "order of Melchizedek," it makes sense to me that he established the celebration of communion using the same elements that Melchizedek used with Abraham, as the man through whom the covenant of God's salvation was confirmed. It is quite reasonable to see the prophetic connection between the meeting between Abraham and Melchizedek and the Lord's Supper. Furthermore, this interpretation has theological and biblical support, in light of the passages in Hebrews that describe Jesus sharing in the same priesthood as Melchizedek. This connection is not a coincidence.

I think it is not wise to ignore the connection between two passages more than two thousand years apart because it would deny the power of God to use historical events for prophetic purposes. I believe that the "bread and wine" that Melchizedek shared with Abraham have a prophetic purpose because, as a forerunner of Christ, Melchizedek established the elements and the method to celebrate the memory of the most significant event in human history, the death of Jesus. I also believe that, as a type and forerunner of Christ, Melchizedek would perform the same acts that would prophetically point to Christ, and in my estimation "the bread and the wine" undoubtedly pointed to Christ.

Someone may object to my interpretation and say that I am reading more into the event than the passage requires or allows. After all, it was just bread and wine, which were two very common items at the time. Although these were common elements in those days, so were meat and many other types of food. While we can say that Melchizedek could have been unaware of the prophetic significance of his act, Jesus certainly was not.

We cannot say that Jesus was unaware of what he was about to do just before his crucifixion, and certainly we cannot say that Jesus was unaware of the celebration that Melchizedek had with Abraham. In my opinion, the theological connection between these two events is undeniable. This is why I believe that the first meeting between Melchizedek and Abraham has eternal value, and Jesus made sure that we recognized this reality when he instituted the Lord's Supper and said, "Do it in remembrance of me" (Lk. 22:19).

Second, apparently, of his own freewill and without being pressured, Abraham gave Melchizedek a tenth of all the loot he had obtained in his military campaigns. Moses did not include any conversations between Abraham and Melchizedek and therefore we do not know how the idea of tithing came about. What we know for sure is that Abraham gave a tenth of his possessions to Melchizedek, after receiving his blessing. Let me share three significant aspects of this exchange.

The first interesting aspect of this exchange is that Abraham started tithing after Melchizedek shared the "bread and wine" with him. This sequence is significant because it indicates that Abraham recognized that Melchizedek, as the high priest of God, was entitled to receive the tithe. And as the writer of Hebrews affirmed, the greater blesses lesser.

The second interesting aspect of the story is that Abraham chose ten percent as his offering for the high priest. Why didn't he choose twenty or even fifty percent? I believe that God revealed the tithe to Abraham. The patriarch did not choose to tithe. God did. When Abraham gave the tenth part to the high priest without being prompted, he showed Melchizedek, himself, and God that he had overcome greed. It is important to note that the next chapter, Genesis 15, God established what we know as the Abrahamic Covenant.

I don't think the theological connection between these two events is a coincidence. Once Abraham accepted the high priesthood of Melchizedek, and had received his blessing, and honored the Lord as his only God with tithe, he was prepared to enter into the everlasting covenant with God.

The third interesting aspect of this event was that Melchizedek accepted Abraham's tithe as if he were entitled to it. That is, in the exchange, Melchizedek did not inform the patriarch that he was wealthy and did not need Abraham's tithe. Not only that, but Melchizedek accepted the tenth as the legitimate amount. I think the reason Melchizedek did not reject the tithe was because the tenth was an issue between God and Abraham. Abraham had to show the Lord that he loved God more than he loved money.

Tithing is in effect today for the same reasons that it was applied to Abraham; we must overcome greed to honor God as the only Lord of our lives. Abraham did not steal from God because he did not appropriate the prerogative that only belongs to God as the only Lord of the universe.

The fact is, the requirement to overcome greed has not changed since Abraham. Like Abraham, we too have to overcome the love of money to begin living in the abundant blessings that God has prepared for those who love him. And like Abraham, God cannot entrust us with more riches and responsibilities until we have overcome our natural selfish tendencies. God has not changed. The purpose of tithing has not changed. And our need to overcome greed is as necessary today as it was four thousand years ago.

It is my conclusion that the meeting between Melchizedek and Abraham had a prophetic meaning related to the two aspects that distinguished the meeting; the "bread and the wine" and the tithe. Both elements are still in force today as part of Abraham's covenant that is fulfilled in Christ and continues with God blessing all the nations through Abraham's seed.

The Tithe and the Mosaic Law

The meeting between Melchizedek and Abraham is an important event because it established the tenth as the means to evaluate people's trustworthiness. In the language of the kingdom, God can only trust people with generous hearts because only this type of person has developed the capacity for compassion and for forgiveness. God revealed the tithe before the Law of Moses went into effect and thus disconnected it from the law. It was important for God that tithing not be seen as coming from the law to avoid, precisely, what has happened, that people would dismiss tithing as a legal requirement that does not apply to the church. If tithing measures people's level of greed, as I have been presenting, then it applies to all people everywhere, for all time. Tithing, as a theological concept, has nothing to do with the Mosaic Law and therefore it did not cease when the cross of Christ replaced the law.

As in the case of Abraham, tithing is an act of faith that identifies the people who have conquered the love of money. As believers, we have a debt of gratitude to Jesus that we pay when we present our tithes and offerings to God. Through Melchizedek, who was the high priest of the Most High God, Jesus appeared to Abraham and celebrated the memorial of his sacrifice with the patriarch. Immediately afterward, in Genesis 15, the Lord appeared to Abraham again and sealed the eternal covenant with the patriarch in blood.

Once Israel became a nation, it needed a system to support the tabernacle, and later the Temple. In Israel, God appointed the Levites to receive the tithe from the people. They were the guardians of the temple and of all religious artifacts. As a result of their selection as guardians of the temple, God did not include the Levites in the inheritance of the distribution of the promised land, precisely so that they did not have conflicts of interest in the administration of Israel's religious life. The rest of the tribes received land to support themselves, but the Levites depended on tithing and their brothers' offerings for their support. The temple and the Lord were their inheritance. In the same way that Melchizedek had the right to Abraham's tithes, the priestly family of Aaron had the right to receive the tithe in the name of God.

The author of the book of Hebrews is very helpful in clarifying this discussion. He said the following regarding Levi and the tithe: "[9] One might even say that Levi himself, who receives tithes, paid tithes through Abraham, [10] for he was still in the loins of his ancestor when Melchizedek met him" (Heb. 7:9-10).

The writer of Hebrews further clarified that Abraham's tithe was more than a simple act of generosity from Abraham to Melchizedek. In reality, Abraham's tithe was a theological imperative that also paid the tithe of those who receive the tithe, the Levites. While some may argue that the writer of Hebrews was speaking figuratively, I disagree. The spiritual significance of the tithe was that Abraham's tithe covered the Levites as temple administrators. As such, Abraham's tithe was not a simple one-time event. On the contrary. Abraham's tithe had a far-reaching and deeper significance. Read with me the instructions that God gave about the children of the Levites: "To the Levites I have given every tithe in Israel for an inheritance, in return for their service that they do, their service in the tent of meeting" (Num. 18:21).

The Levites would receive all the tithes as an inheritance in exchange for their work in the meeting tabernacle and then in the temple. While under the Law, the function of the tithe was to provide for the temple and for those who served there. That role has not changed to this day. Similarly, the purpose of tithing has not changed. Believers are still responsible for showing that we have overcome our love of money. God, to ensure that the Levites also understood this concept, commanded the following:

> Moreover, you shall speak and say to the Levites, 'When you take from the people of Israel the tithe that I have given you from them for your inheritance, then you shall present a contribution from it to the Lord, a tithe of the tithe (Num. 18:26).

This is why the author of the book of Hebrews tells us that when Abraham tithed to Melchizedek, he was symbolically tithing on behalf of the Levites. The Levites, in turn, became the legitimate heirs of the tithe. However, even though the Levites could legitimately receive the tithe, they were not exempt from tithing. Abraham's tithe to Melchizedek entitled the Levites to receive a tithe from the people, but even after that, they were required to pay their own tithe. Everyone owes tithing, because every individual must conquer greed.

Many people have asked, if God does not need our money to accomplish his purposes, why does he require tithing? The Bible provides two responses to God's demand for tithing. First, tithing is not for God's benefit. As I have said before, overcoming greed or the love of money is a prerequisite to reestablish a transparent relationship with God. Therefore, God designed the tithe as the mechanism for us to make an honest evaluation to break the cycle of greed.

The second part of the answer is that God created us to have fellowship with him. God's desire to fellowship with us is so deep that he was willing to experience the pains of physical death to reconcile us with him. If greed separates us from God, then, we have to think of the tithe as the instruments that eliminates idolatry from our hearts. Only then we can be free for fellowship with God. Thus, I believe that tithing affirms God's purpose in making us active partners in his saving plan. If we are not faithful with our own tithes, God cannot entrust us with greater responsibilities in his saving mission. The apostle Paul even said that we are partners with God in the work of the gospel (1 Cor. 3: 9).

The apostle rebuked the Corinthians for the divisions they had created within the church. Paul wanted to clarify that divisions were a waste of time because we are all coworkers of God. His message that we belong to God was quite clear. However, the other aspect of the statement was that God called us to minister on his behalf. We do the God's work, not because he cannot do it. On the contrary. We do God's work because he has chosen to achieve his purposes through human means. We tithe as partners of God in the work of the kingdom, and we need to trust God, and he wants to trust us. Therefore, we tithe.

Furthermore, when people oppose the tithe, or offerings in general, they are in effect saying that they are not interested in partnering with God to achieve his eternal purposes. We observe this same phenomenon when some Christians say that they do not need to join a local church to be Christians. Actually, they need to join a local church because God's mission is accomplished within and through the local church. The same goes for tithing. God uses our generosity, which is the primary evidence that we are overcoming the idolatry of the love of money in order to bless others through the mission of the church.

Many years ago, a business partner told a group of people at a training session, "Show me your checkbook, and I'll show you your priorities." Most of us have a hard time setting healthy priorities, even when we want to obey God. This is the constant struggle that we must overcome to follow Jesus. I am sure that many people confess that they love God, but when we ask them to also love their neighbor, they return to the legalistic mentality and ask Jesus, "and who is my neighbor" (Lk. 10:25-37). It is our calling and duty to strive to defeat the idols in our lives and to partner with God to reach the lost.

A lawyer's question in Luke 10:25 led Jesus to offer the parable of the Good Samaritan, who helped a wounded man lying on the side of the road and paid all his expenses until he had fully recovered. Our neighbor is anyone who needs our compassion. The love of God does not exist in a vacuum and it must always find expression through our relationships with other people. The faster we learn this lesson, the faster we can stop making excuses not to join the local church and support its mission with our finances.

If people want an opportunity to make a difference in God's plan, they can start by giving him the tithe that can have a transformational effect for the kingdom. One of the things I have learned from Scripture over the years is that as people become more faithful, God expands their influence to reach many more people. A man named Jabez prayed for the Lord to bless him and to "enlarge [his] border" (1 Chr. 4:10). The writer told us that God granted his request. Jabez wanted to have greater influence, and God trusted that he would use that influence to bless other, not simply to enrich himself. Maybe, all of us should pray like Jabez and ask the Lord to enlarge our borders.

As I have said before, we can always go ahead and do our own thing. We can choose to live independent of God and to take our own chances in a random world. That's each person's prerogative. God gave us freedom of the will to make our own moral choices, our own mistakes, and experience the consequences, good and bad, of those choices. Or we can choose to be reconciled with Him. Since God is gracious and good, people always have the opportunity to reverse course, repent, and return to God. This was God's cry for the people of Israel in the context of the tithe, "return to me, and I will return to you" (Mal. 3:7).

The Tithe is Not a Money Matter

One of the worst interpretations of tithing is to say that it is a money matter. Many televangelists and con men have preached the tithe as a financial transaction between God and people. The thinking is that God needs our money to invest in his kingdom or he might be running out of funds at any time. Do you know who is running out of funds? The money changers in the temple, that's who. God's call for the tithe has nothing to do with God's resourcefulness to accomplish his mission.

Beloved brothers and sisters, tithing is a matter of the heart. To the extent that people think tithing is an expense of their money, they will never give with joy and will never experience God's financial blessings in in return. When Christian view the tithe as one more debt, it is difficult to give with joy in our hearts. Nobody, as far as I know, sends extra money when they pay their bills. People who do not tithe may have moments of financial increase because they were smart enough to get a hold of a good paying job. But they will never fully enjoy the blessing of transforming someone's life in the name of Christ. To the extent that people think tithing is about their money, when they don't own anything, to that extent they will miss finding satisfaction in witnessing God's magnificent grace. And to the extent people believe that tithing is about their money, they will fail to understand God's purpose for their lives.

So what is tithing? Tithing is one-tenth of your increase (salary or income), and the tithe belongs to the LORD. If we really want to accept what the word of God prescribes, that is, if the word of God is an actual command from God, then the tithe does not belong to us to do with as we please. Actually, if we keep the tithe, we are playing with someone else's possessions. Listen to Moses:

> You may not eat within your towns the tithe of your grain or of your wine or of your oil, or the firstborn of your herd or of your flock, or any of your vow offerings that you vow, or your freewill offerings or the contribution that you present, [18] but you shall eat them before the Lord your God in the place that the Lord your God will choose, you and your son and your daughter, your male servant and your female servant, and the Levite who is within your towns. And you shall rejoice before the Lord your God in all that you undertake. [19] Take care that you do not neglect the Levite as long as you live in your land (Deut. 12:17-20).

Our increase is our income. We must give a tithe from all we receive because the tithe belongs to the Lord. It's sacred to God. But please do not forget the principle we have shared repeatedly in this short book—the tithe belongs to God because it is the remedy that frees us from serving Mammon. With the tithe God is protecting us from idol worship and from all kinds of evil. So, the tithe is for our sakes, not his. Never forget this profound message. Moses added the following: "Every tithe of the land, whether of the seed of the land or of the fruit of the trees, is the Lord's; it is holy to the Lord" (Lev. 27:30).

The tithe belongs to God. Some could object by saying that those texts are inside the books of the law. And they're perfectly right in that observation, with one problem. The tithe did not originate with the law, and therefore, it could not have expired with the law. The tithe was, and is, about each person who is seeking intimacy with God without the distraction of the love of money. It is the instrument God uses to cleanse us from greed.

Just as the New Testament epistles define Christ's message to the church today, the law defined God's requirements for Israel, but Moses did not institute the tithe. He defined the utility of something that had already been instituted when Abraham gave the tenth of his spoils of war to Melchizedek. Unless there is a different pattern that contradicts Abraham's pattern, it is more prudent to accept that God has the same expectation of us that he had of Abraham. That is, Abraham had accepted the lordship of God the creator of the universe, and he responded with the tithe as evidence that he had overcome greed and that the Lord was his only God. We must remember that until that time Abraham had not given a tithe to anyone, nor did he have any intentions of doing so. However, when he met the High Priest of Salem (who was a type of Christ), Abraham did not hesitate in giving him the tenth of all his possessions without hesitation. We should respond to Jesus's lordship over our lives with the same generosity.

Some people have asked me if it's appropriate to tithe their time. Normally, this means they, either don't understand the purpose of the tithe, or don't know how churches function. In addition to all the benefits of the tithe, we need to teach our members that offering our time is similar to Cain's offering because it is inadequate to fulfill God's purposes. The readers remember Cain's story. God demanded a blood sacrifice to atone for sins, but Cain decided to bring to the Lord a grain offering. An atonement offering requires blood, and a grain offering was insufficient. Cain, who proved he was a carnal man, was not ready to make a sin confession to the Lord and to offer a legitimate sacrifice. For obvious reasons, the Lord did not accept Cain's offering. His offering was a an afront to the prophecy of Jesus's death on the cross.

If you are wondering how Cain dismissed the prophecy about Jesus, do not lose too much sleep on this. Cain did not have to know all the details of the prophetic message to obey. Abel certainly knew that he had to make a blood sacrifice in obedience to the Lord, and we know that Cain and Able were grown men. They had seen and had participated in sacrifices before. Thus, they understood what God required. We know, and Cain knew, that God's prophetic message was almost always communicated through events and people's responses to those events. Cain did not have to know all the details of the prophetic message. All he needed to know was that the Lord had demanded a blood sacrifice, and that he was called to obey, not to question the Lord's commandments. The Lord rejected Cain's offering because he offered the Lord what he wanted and not what the Lord had demanded from him.

As we consider Cain's attitude, we find that his heart was away from God and, instead of repenting before the Lord, he killed his own brother (Gen. 4:1-10). Those who want to tithe their time are not bringing to the Lord from their increase because we do not own or earn time. Actually, the only way to measure time is as a decrease, not an increase. As such, tithing our time is bringing a defective offering to cover up our love of money. In this sense, these individuals' offerings are not any better than Cain's. They may actually be worse. At least Cain had to work to grow the crops he offered.

The Lord does not only command the giving of the tithe, he has also stated the tithe already belongs to him. People have misunderstood God's commandments for centuries as being burdensome. Unbelievers and believers alike have the tendency to interpret God's commandments as restrictions and impositions that punish us or take away our freedoms. They ignore that God's commandments, as Jesus said, are not onerous. He said, "for my yoke is easy, and my burden is light" (Matt. 11:30). When we have a proper understanding of God's commandments, we do not find them burdensome. They are a blessing. The commandment regarding the tithe has the same intent, to protect us from ourselves. Read it with me. "Bring all tithes to the storehouse so that there may be food in my house" (Mal. 3:10).

The Good News Translation Bible says: "Bring the full amount of your tithes to the Temple, so that there will be plenty of food there." We need to understand that God does not eat, nor does he need us to provide him with food (Ps. 50:12). The food is for those who work in the temple. During Malachi's time the Levites and priests resided in God's house. They received the tithe as evidence that the people of Israel had partnered with God in his mission. Today, our bishops, elders, and pastors, who shepherd the flock of God and serve in the congregations, are the legitimate recipients of the tithe.

The New Testament added another requirement for the tithe: to provide for widows and orphans (Acts 6:1). The Apostles would continue to receive support for their livelihood, but other leaders would be responsible for assessing the needs of the believing community, and they had to distribute the funds according to those needs.

NOTE: There is another problem in today's church—some deacons have been incorrectly given the responsibility of dealing with disciplinary or pastoral matters (roles that only properly belong to Bishops, Elders, and Pastors). This error has distorted the deacons' function in the church. Instead of serving tables or ensuring the economic needs of the community are met, in many traditions they have become *de facto* owners of their churches, to include developing the attitude of controlling and manipulating pastors with threats of firing or of reducing their salaries. To say it bluntly—some traditions have elected lovers of money to positions of service. This has been a disaster for many churches. The arrangement of deacons as church owners does not work because ministry cannot function through greed and idolatry.

Practical Applications for the Tithe

Believers bring the tithe to the church. In the same way the Levites were the only legitimate recipients of the tithe, bishops, elders, and pastors are the only legitimate receivers of the tithe for the church. Once people bring the tithe to the church, they cannot reclaim it as their own. It belongs to God. This is the reason it is necessary for pastors and leaders to be men of character, respectable, with honor and integrity. When church leaders are trustworthy, the members can be confident they are fulfilling God's purpose for the tithe and are not simply making "shameful gain" (1 Pet. 5:2).

Tithers do not determine how the church spends their gifts. However, church leaders, at all levels, must be mindful to protect people's faithfulness with their tithes to God's kingdom. We must remember that we are partnering with the Lord and with the local pastor to extend God's kingdom, not to extend the local pastor's influence. The local pastor must be accountable to the church for his actions, to include how he uses the resources God has entrusted for him to administer. That said, the tither cannot choose to use God's money for personal projects. In other words, the tithe is so that "there is food in [the Lord's] house."

Someone can ask, what should people do if the local church doesn't use the tithe properly? To address and minimize this concern, all church business sessions must be open to the public. All decisions have to be made by a leadership that respect the pastor's vision and mission for the church, as well as advocates for the needs and priorities of the different ministries in the church. Church leaders must publish an annual budget that is available to the public. If people choose not to see the budget that's their prerogative. These processes are used to ensure transparency with God's finances. If people do not know what's going on, it should not be because the information is not available.

Let's Revisit the Agricultural System

The fact that we live in an agricultural system means that whatever happens on this world depends on the principle of "seedtime and harvest." Additionally, the agricultural system principle sets in stone how we receive the benefits and consequences of our moral decisions and actions. The law of the seed and harvest is one of the principal tools God uses for assessing people's commitment to Christ and their ability to rid themselves of greed, which is a form of idolatry (Col. 3:5).

It is important to note that the tithe to God's work is the key that opens the unlocks God's financial blessings and breaks the cycle of greed. But the tithe, itself, does not open the financial blessing. The tithe reveals that we have overcome greed, and it is this fact that let's God *know* that we are ready to handle God's abundance. Thus, the tithe is the physical manifestation of a life that has overcome the love of money. Many Christians who resist giving their tithe to the church have a significant misunderstanding of how God's agricultural system actually works. I want to share some basic keys that can help us understand the seedtime and harvest cycle.

First key: God Provides The Seed And Grows The Harvest

Agricultural systems are strictly based on the seedtime and harvest cycle. This cycle is as rigid as the law of gravity. Churches and church leaders cannot make financial decisions that may run counter to the harvest cycle. A cycle is a series of events that repeat in the same order and in the same intervals every time. Systems are predictable and repeatable. They are easy to replicate and become universally available. Since God created the world as an agricultural system, this means that people cannot expect to receive something for which they have not planted a seed. But it also means that we will receive the results or consequences of our decisions, regardless of whether they are physical or spiritual. Thus, a murderer will receive the harvest of his action, even if he was not aware that his actions represented a seed that would give a fruit.

The agricultural cycle is true for everything we do in this world. The birth cycle of a child is 270 days of gestation. The corn cycle is approximately 125 days. The human life cycle is about 70 years or 80 for the strongest among us. Everyone goes through the same process. God is responsible for providing the seeds for the sower and he is responsible for the multiplication of the harvest, but each individual takes responsibilities for plowing the fields, choosing the seed they sow, and watering the soil. Read with me:

> He who supplies seed to the sower and bread for food will supply and multiply your seed for sowing and increase the harvest of your righteousness (2 Cor. 9:10).

Believers must remember that everything we have comes from God. It is also necessary to note that even though God provides the seed for sowing, the harvest is directly related to the choices we make with the seed. That is, when we sow into God's kingdom, God will bless our good works. God knows our weaknesses. He knows how much we struggle with selfishness, envy, and greed, and yet, when we sow seeds of righteousness, God is faithful to give us a harvest of grace. In this context our generosity is the external evidence of our righteousness. The apostle Paul added that we are generous in our giving, we "will be enriched in every way to be generous in every way" (2 Cor. 9:11). Paul's argument was that joyful giving opens God's blessing with the expressed purpose to bless others, and our generosity with others produces "thanksgiving to God" (2 Cor. 9:12). Probably, there is nothing that reveals selfishness, envy, and greed more than the love of money. Those who trust God would agree with the apostle James's statement.

> Every good gift and every perfect gift is from above, coming down from the Father of lights, with whom there is no variation or shadow due to change (Jam. 1:17).

Even our skills and opportunities to earn a living come from God. Whether we like it or not, God is interested in our wallets because our attitude towards money determines our level of loyalty to him. Additionally, our loyalty in money management reveals whether we are trustworthy to receive greater responsibility. We all know the parable that the Lord Jesus said about the servants who received some talents (Matt. 25:14-30).

A wealthy man went far away and gave his servants three his goods to manage. He gave one of the servants five talents. He gave another two. And to the third servant he gave one a talent. The money these servants received was not theirs. Thee servant could manage their talents in any way they saw fit by making their own decisions, but upon their lord's return, each of the servants had to account for how they had managed the assets of their master.

After some time had passed, the rich man returned from his trip and called his servants to receive their reports with any financial gains they might have accumulated. The servant who received five talents brought a gain of five talents more, and he received the appreciation of his lord. The same happened with the servant who received two talents. He also multiplied his talents and gave four talents to his lord. But the third servant was lazy, and he buried his talent. When his lord returned the third servant had not earned anything. His lord's response was severe. He called him an "evil and negligent servant" (Matt. 24:26).

The parable of the talents was about life. The Lord created us with certain skills and talents that we must put into action in our lives because God is going to call us to account one day. On that day we will have to give an explanation of how our lives were of benefit to the kingdom of God. Many people are wasting their lives and when the day of accountability comes, they will have nothing to present to the Lord.

The parable concluded with the rich man taking the talent from the servant who did not produce anything, and he gave it to the one who had multiplied his five talents. The former had wasted his opportunity, but the latter had earned his master's trust. The meaning of this parable goes beyond financial management, but it includes our fidelity to manage someone else's assets, in this case, those assets are God's gifts. Please do not ignore two revelations in this passage.

The first revelation every Christian must know is that everything we have belongs to God. When we tithe, we are not giving to God something that we own. We are giving God something that belongs to him, for everything belongs to God. When we keep ninety percent, we are not keeping something that belongs to us. Rather, we are keeping something that already belongs to God. The ninety percent we keep is God's blessing us for breaking the barrier of greed. It is unwise to think that we can keep the tithe for ourselves and at the same time expect that God would praise our actions.

The second revelation every Christian must know is that if we mismanage the talents the Lord bestowed upon us he cannot bless us in the way that he desires. When we neglect our responsibilities regarding the tithe, the Lord cannot expand our borders of influence. If we cannot even be faithful in the smallest things, we should not expect God to trust the bigger things into our hands.

If God is not the Lord of our wallets, then he is not our only God. But, we must acknowledge that the God of the Bible is exclusive, and he does not share his glory. He does not transfer his prerogatives to false, mute, and blind gods created by human greed and depravity. The Bible declares that the "love of money is the root of all kinds of evils." Since this is the case, God does not want us to waste our lives worshipping at the altar of the mighty dollar. Remember that the law of the harvest states that the one who sows generously will have a bountiful harvest (2 Cor. 9:6). Look with me at how Paul closed this section in verse eleven: "You will be enriched in every way to be generous in every way, which through us will produce thanksgiving to God" (2 Cor. 9:11).

Second Key: Financial Reciprocity

The simplest definition of the law of financial reciprocity indicates that God always returns a blessing that is more generous than our offerings. The Lord Jesus illustrated this principle in Luke 6. Let's read it.

> Give, and it will be given to you; good measure, pressed down, shaken together and running over, will they give into your lap; because with the same measure with which you measure, they will measure you again (Lk. 6:38).

The immediate context of this passage refers to loving our enemies and doing good (Lk. 6:35). The Lord included a commandment to lend money without expecting anything in return. Then the Lord made a surprising statement. If we lend without expecting anything in return "our reward will be great, and we will be called sons of God" (Lk. 6:35b). The Lord Jesus connected generosity with being called "children of God." This is, without a doubt, one of those statements that take us by surprise because it presents a direct connection between having a generous heart with receiving God's approval.

The Lord continued his teaching by saying, "Be ye therefore merciful, even as your Father is merciful" (Lk. 6:36). This declaration of the Lord is profound because it makes another connection between generosity and mercy. Normally, most of us don't see how generosity and mercy are related. But the Lord put the two words in the same context to show that the same attitude that moves people to generosity, also motivates them to be merciful.

The Lord also contrasted "judging and condemning" with forgiving and being generous. I think Jesus was discussing two different attitudes. On the one hand, Jesus introduced a judgmental attitude that led to condemning others. When the Bible demands that we not judge other people, almost always, it is in reference to making superficial judgments based on external appearances. This judgmental attitude invariably leads individuals to be more condemning and less merciful.

On the other hand, the Lord introduced a forgiving attitude as it proceeded from generosity. That is, we can know if when people have compassion and exhibit a forgiving attitude when they are generous with their money in supporting God's work and those in need. In the v. 37 the Lord spoke of forgiveness, and in v. 38 he spoke of generosity as if these two attitudes of the heart were connected. I think Jesus connected these two attitudes to indicate that when we overcome greed and become generous, inevitably will make us more compassionate.

In the words of the Lord Jesus, generosity has two immediate results. First is that "we are children of God." Second, generosity is the only character quality in this context that has a promise of abundant blessings. The generous believer will receive "good measure, pressed down, shaken, and overflowing that they will give into your lap." God's promises regarding generosity are spectacular and giving is the only activity that receives a promise of blessings until they abound.

The apostle Paul echoed the words of Christ when he said that "Each one should give as he proposed in his heart: not with sadness, nor out of necessity, because God loves the cheerful giver" (2 Cor. 9:7). It is not only necessary to give generously, but the Lord also prefers that we give with joy. The apostle Paul stated that generous people do not give reluctantly or under compulsion.

Many biblical pastors and scholars have used this passage to argue that tithing is not necessary in the church today. Their argument is quite simple: God's requirement is that people give with joy according to what they have proposed in their hearts. I fully agree that God wants us to be joyful givers. However, I don't think anyone can give joyfully if they haven't conquered greed, for obvious reasons. As long as Christians are struggling to overcome their love of money, the idea that they can give joyfully is an illusion. While I agree that we should give joyfully, I also believe that overcoming greed is the prerequisite for joyful giving.

One of the greatest benefits of giving generously is that God has promised to reward our generosity with overflowing blessings. As we know, God is a farmer, and he operates through the seed and harvest cycle. The blessings that come from God include wisdom, finances, protection of our property that will result in praises to God. I believe that since this world is an agricultural system, even unbelievers receive a blessed when they put into practice the law of sowing and reaping. However, the blessings unbelievers receive serve as elements of judgment because they do not acknowledge they received their blessings from God. When unbelievers receive a blessing for their

80

efforts, their hearts become hardened against the Lord because they convince themselves that God is irrelevant for their success.

Every believer must know that God only accepts the offering presented according to his purpose. He has promised to give us more than we need, but not because we deserve it. It is out of his abundant grace that God created this system with a built-in generous harvest mechanism. God wants the world to glorify him for our benefit. Whenever we replace God as the Lord of their lives with other idols, we are the ones who suffer. God does not stop being God, but we lose access to our Source of life and blessing. Let me make three additional observations.

First of all, from God's perspective, taking a tenth of our income to the church is not optional, but not because God will force us to comply. The tithe is not optional in that our failure breaks our fellowship with God and we miss out on God's blessings in our lives. If I read Malachi correctly, the people had abandoned God's commandments and the evidence of their rebellion was that they were withholding the tithe. Therefore, the first visible evidence that the people had returned to God was their obedience in the tithe. As I discussed in Chapter One, withholding the tithe is theft, but not because we have broken into God's safe. It is a robbery because we have presumed to have the right to a divine prerogative.

Second, we must remember that when we bring the full tithe to God's house, he is obligated, by his own word to "open the windows of heaven" to shower us with his favor.

Third, God challenged us to test him with the tithe. This passage in Malachi is the only place in all of God's revelation that gave permission to the people to test the Lord. The Bible has several warnings against testing or tempting God. Testing God is something people simply did not do. God considered it to be a great offense when people tested his patience, his power, or his divinity. But when God spoke about tithing, the prophet told us that God wanted us to "test

[him] with the [tithing]." God's challenge to the people was that if we don't believe in his promises, we can put them to the test. Tithing is the only place in the Bible where challenging God is not only acceptable, it is encouraged.

The Law of God's Provision

The law of God's provision is simple: God has promised to meet all our needs. If God dresses the lilies of the field more splendidly than King Solomon clothed himself, no doubt he will take care of us who are more valuable to them (Matt. 6:28-29). Let me clarify that Jesus did not promise to satisfy all our desires. He promised to satisfy all our needs. Although Christians often refer to God's provisions as a promise to satisfy our cravings, the reality is very different. The interesting aspect about this law is that when we are faithful with our tithes, God always responds with more than we need or asked. Believers who have conquered greed and are living free from the idolatry caused by the love of money, perfectly understand that our generosity is a seed that will produce an abundant harvest.

Psalm 23 is one of the most often quoted psalms in the Bible. Most people have memorized the first part of the first verse of this psalm: "The Lord is my shepherd." The second part of the verse is not cited with the same frequency, but it goes to the heart of our discussion. We know that the Lord is our Good Shepherd precisely because he promised that "I will lack anything" in my life. We are sure of the goodness of the Good Shepherd because we have experienced his actions on our behalf. If we do a detailed study of the scriptures we find that God's grace has always been manifested in abundance for those who are faithful to the Lord.

Without a doubt, the Bible promises that God will provide for his children. But many believers have understood God's promise as a blanket statement that God is obligated to protects us from all suffering and prevents us from experiencing financial struggles. We must

82

understand that God's focus is on fulfilling his eternal purpose for us. This purpose has many twists and turns, and on many occasions, God does not fill-in all the details of what we are going through.

On the one hand, he will provide all our physical needs, but if we want to live in abundance we need to use God's blessings for the well-being of the community of faith. On the other hand, God's primary concern is getting us to conform to the image of Christ (Rom. 8:29). Let me add here that Christ is the prototype of man who lives according to the will of the Eternal Father, and when we become like him, we can experience the greatest blessing, which is to live in the presence of God without fear and anxiety.

Some believers may then ask: How do we know when or how God will meet our physical and financial needs? This is, of course, a very legitimate question, and the answer can be a bit tricky. I don't think I can come up with an answer that will satisfy all readers, but perhaps the readers are curious enough to study the subject in more detail in the future.

I would suggest that the best way to understand God's provisions is to break them down into three levels. First of all, believers must prioritize our relationship with the Lord starting with our confession that he is the only Lord of our lives. On this first level, Christians must overcome worldly temptations, especially the love of money, because greed is the most pernicious expression of idolatry that afflicts the church today. Once we have conquered the love of money, we can move to the second level of God's provisions.

At the second level I suggest that once we have conquered greed, we begin to make a total commitment where we will prioritize expanding the kingdom of God using our financial resources and our time. At this level we are living in obedience to a call from God that transcends our most immediate needs. It goes without saying that when the kingdom of God is our highest priority, God will respond to our faithfulness by providing beyond what we need. In the second level of commitment the Lord can trust our abilities to manage our finances faithfully, and then he entrust us to manage the finances of other believers who need to grow to our level of commitment. Additionally, at this level we are examples of faith for other Christians and for the world, and we are living comfortably, but we have not yet reached transformative abundance. Read with me the apostle Paul's encouragement to the Philippians church:

> [11]I am not saying this because I have a shortage, because I have learned to be content, whatever my situation may be. [12]I know how to live humbly, and I know how to have abundance; in everything and for everything I am taught, so to be satiated as to be hungry, so to have abundance as to suffer need. [13]I can do everything in Christ who strengthens me (Phil. 4:11-13).

When we are content with God's provision regardless of our current circumstances. I am not suggesting that God takes away our blessings. On the contrary. I am suggesting that when we have undergone a transformation in which our intimacy with God is our greatest glory and joy, nothing physical or material is important. We are living abundantly, but we measure our blessings through our friendship with the Lord, and we can walk in peace within our circumstances. At this level we have our attitude is so in tune with the purposes of God that even abundant life no longer motivates us.

At the third level of commitment is where we can drive a Ferrari, own a fifteen-bedroom house, have ten million dollars in the bank, and those things do not have a negative influence on how we relate to God, to the church, and to the other people. Also, at this level we can lose everything, find ourselves living in a hut, and our relationship with God and with the church will not be affected, because the Lord has become our lot in life. This was Job's level. He lost his fortune, his family, and his health, and he could still say: "I know my Redeemer lives, and I will see him in my flesh" (Job 19:25-27). There is a deep acceptance that our lives belong to the Lord, and we can join the words of the apostle Paul when he said: "Well, if we live, we live for the Lord; and if we die, for the Lord we die. So, whether we live, or die, we are the

Lord's" (Rom. 14:8). The apostle also added that "for me to live is Christ, and to die is gain" (Phil. 1:21). Very few of us reach this level, but most of us who make a full commitment to the Lord will come very close, and this process begins with tithing to break the chains of greed in our lives.

The Law of Abundance

Jesus said, "Give, and it will be given to you; good measure, pressed down, shaken together and running over, will they give into your lap; for with the same measure that you measure, they will measure you again" (Lk. 6:38). As with all of God's promises, Jesus promised that he will respond to our generosity with more than we need. Since God is generous, he cannot help but bless us with excessive abundance. In other words, the creator of heaven and earth, the eternal Logos of God, the alpha and the Omega, has said, and I quote: "But seek first the kingdom of God and his righteousness, and all these things will be added to you" (Matt. 6:33). If we have our priorities in the correct order, God will spare no effort to give us everything, and more, than we need.

I want to take a closer look at the passage from Luke, which I mentioned earlier, from a theological perspective. Although many commentators have mentioned that Jesus's statements in this passage appear to be independent of one another, I think Jesus was grouping types of attitudes. The first group had negative commandments, and the second group had positive commandments that illustrate that greed and generosity have two different attitudes or starting points. Let's take a look at them.

In the first set, Jesus said, "Do not judge, and you will not be judged" (Lk. 6:27a). This statement by Jesus does not mean that we cannot evaluate the behaviors or characters of other people. Jesus's concern was that we judge other people without expressing grace or without having accurate information. At best, our efforts to judge other people's spiritual journeys are an exercise in prejudice and self-righteousness. God, who judges the deepest thoughts of the people, does not prejudge the motives of the people. Despite the fact that he already has exhaustive information on people's attitudes, he judges with mercy after giving us the opportunity to repent, to do things well and to have the opportunity to reconcile with him. God never rushes to make judgments, but human beings are prone to make hasty decisions, and often without precise information about the subject of our just indignation. This type of prejudice is an attitude of the heart that makes some people feel superior to others.

A similar sentiment is present in Jesus's second warning: "Do not condemn, and you will not be condemned" (Lk. 6:37b). Like the first admonition, Jesus was not prohibiting the passing of sentences against people who were guilty of a crime or crime. Christians can evaluate (judge) situations and people based on physical evidence, but the Lord forbade us to judge the intentions of the heart. The same is true with condemning. We can condemn harmful behavior, but we cannot make judgments of the eternal state or the condition of people's hearts. I think this first set identifies the attitude of a person dominated by greed. Some of you may wonder, Bishop, how did you come to that conclusion? Keep reading.

Jesus, without interrupting his train of thought, moved to the second set of attitudes. I found Jesus's words extremely profound. He said: "Forgive, and you will be forgiven; give, and it will be given to you" (Lk. 6:37b-38a). While most commentators suggest that Jesus simply made four independent statements that have no connection to each other, I cannot accept this conclusion for a simple reason. It is doubtful that Lucas, who was a highly educated physician and also a meticulous historian, wrote a series of statements in the same context without having a logical connection to each other.

In this context, I think Lucas grouped two sets of statements that identified two particular attitudes related to people's attitudes about money. That is why Luke concluded the presentation of Christ by

86

speaking of generosity and the agricultural cycle of this world. It is necessary to add that the only commandment that received an explanation and expansion was the commandment to give generously. For me, this is an indication that Jesus wanted to detail the attitudes that exist behind the actions mentioned in the context. The first group identified people who prejudge and condemn the spiritual condition of the people. This type of person is not very generous because they have difficulties extending grace and mercy to others. The second group identified that people who have mercy know how to person, and their generosity is the evidence of their spiritual attitude. This second group does not prejudge or condemn people because we understand that judgment belongs to the Lord.

It is my conviction that people with attitudes of prejudging and condemning others suffer from deficiency of grace and mercy. In my opinion, it is crucial to understand that merciful people do not prejudge and do not condemn the condition of the hearts and attitudes of others. I would say that without grace and without mercy people cannot be generous.

On the other hand, I propose that people who have forgiving hearts will also have generous hearts, and vice versa. I cannot overlook the importance that generosity has in this context because the only statement Jesus extended to was about generosity. The other three attitudes left them without comment. However, read with me how Jesus described the benefits of giving generously. When we give, God will respond with "good measure, pressed down, shaken together, and overflowing they will give into your lap" (Lk. 6:38). In other words, God responds to the generous person with blessings that are far beyond what is expected. If we are generous with our money, with our mercy, with our love and with compassion, we will receive an abundance of those same attitudes. Similarly, the downside of this equation is also true. If people are quick in prejudging others, they will also receive judgment in the same measure that they measured their neighbor.

The four descriptions are attitudes or conditions of the heart. Some people have overcome prejudiced attitudes and have begun to experience God's abundant blessings in their lives. Others have remained attached to their sinful nature, or remain immature Christians, and have been unable to enjoy God's abundant blessings for their lives.

Without a doubt, forgiveness is an attitude that comes from a repentant heart that understands that God forgave us first. Until we learn to forgive others, we will not be able to experience God's forgiveness properly in our own lives. The former is a significant statement because it points to the preceding verse in Luke 6:36, where he said, "Be ye therefore merciful, even as your Father is merciful" (Lk. 6:36). Jesus was evaluating our attitudes in these four areas of our character to see how closely we are related to the merciful character of God. The Lord gave us a warning in the form of negative commandments to correct our tendency to be overly arrogant and legalistic.

I add that prejudicial and condemning attitudes are a sign of spiritual immaturity. Spiritual immaturity is a reference to Christians who have not yet assimilated the transformative power that God's grace has on their souls. Those who are not spiritually developed have not understood the character of God and do not understand the grace and generous heart of God, regardless of how long they have been in the church. Those who are more spiritually mature understand that Jesus gave us two parameters that identify how we are progressing in grace and generosity. They go hand in hand. Our ability to forgive others is manifested through our generosity, and generous people have develop the ability to forgive.

I think Luke left us two practical truths to understand God's character. First, God is forgiving and generous, and he expects believers in Christ to imitate these two divine qualities. We know that God forgave our sins when he gave us his Son to die in our place. I dare say that a person who has difficulties forgiving others has not yet conquered their greed because mercy is both an act of grace and an act

88

of generosity. By this I do not mean that these people are not making progress. But I do want to say that they still have a way to go until they reach the measure of Christ.

Second, Lucas also told us that if we genuinely believe God as we claim, then we will be generous with our money with the full assurance that God will reward us beyond what we can imagine. The Bible has countless passages that affirm that God is fully committed to providing for the needs of those who sow in the kingdom. I will mention two here:

> Honor the Lord with thy riches, with the first fruits of all thy crops; then your barns will fill up to overflow (Prov. 3:9-10).

> There are those who distribute, and more are added to them; And there are those who retain more than is fair, but they come to poverty. The generous soul will be prospered; And he that satiates, he shall also be satisfied (Prov. 11:24-25).

God Opens the Windows of Heaven

I have argued that tithing is the key that opens the windows of heaven. In other words, tithing breaks the craving for more possessions, regardless of their usefulness. It is like breaking an addiction. The alcoholic wants more alcohol because he craves it, not because he needs it. Greed has the same effect on people.

Greed has two nefarious effects on people. On the one hand, greed causes people to become self-centered and selfish. This attitude prevents these people from sharing with others and enjoying the benefits of receiving fruits from seeds sown in other people's lives. On the other hand, greed prevents people from understanding that the best way to increase their spiritual wealth is by sowing financial seeds in other people's lives. Our tithes are the simplest and most basic act of sowing spiritual seeds in God's kingdom and other people.

God opens the windows of heaven when the individual understands that material possessions, including money, are transitory and that only eternal things have lasting value. When I say that an individual cannot begin to value eternal things until he has broken the cycle of greed, I mean that the love of money prevents us from appreciating spiritual truths, because idolatry has a blinding effect on God's attributes. But when we give God what is rightfully his, there is an added benefit. We begin to notice that we always have more than we need.

Let me add another spiritual secret here. Our attitudes about money extend to other areas of our lives. This means that when money is our object of affection, our relationships with our families and friends, our jobs, and our expectations for the future will be adversely affected. This principle is evident with the wealthy ruler, who preferred to lose eternal life to divest himself of his money. We can also see the same principle, but in its positive form, with the poor widow who gave everything she had and received the approval of Jesus for having a generous heart.

I believe that many churches are in financial difficulties because believers have not conquered greed. I can say it in another way. Christians have not overcome the selfish factor or human tendency to care for "#1" without considering the broader impact that these decisions may have on the Body of Christ.

The Divine Purpose of God's Revelation

I believe that everything the Bible describes has divine purposes. Biblical writers captured the revelation of God through historical events so that we can have a point of reference in the knowledge of God. In the same way that it is not possible to have a relationship of emotional intimacy with strangers, neither can we have spiritual intimacy with God if we do not know who he is. It was necessary, then, that God made himself known using historical interactions so that we could understand the most basic elements of his character. This is the reason I believe that all the events recorded in the Bible are intended to move us toward God. Since the fall of Adam and Eve, humanity has been on a journey away from God. At the same time, the Lord has done everything possible to bring us back to him.

For generations, God has used men and women who willingly listen to his voice and faithfully recorded the personality qualities that define him. We can understand God's character qualities because we share most of them with him. When God imparted his spirit to Adam (Gen. 2:18), he shared with the first man the relational capacities that enabled him to have communion with God on a spiritual and emotional level. Our personhood qualities give us an intrinsic connection with other people and with God. Since we come from God, and he is our source of life, we cannot survive without him. Therefore, the Bible reveals that we can be restored to a relationship of spiritual intimacy with God.

It is our personhood connection to God that makes biblical revelation so essential to our lives. If God had chosen to remain in the shadows, we would never have known him. But he wanted to make himself known and I believe God created us to have fellowship with us. More importantly, God wants to share his kingdom with us, making us joint heirs with Christ of all the blessings of heaven.

These two aspects of God's design for humanity are rooted in God's love. All the character qualities associated with love, such as grace, compassion, mercy, and forgiveness, can only find expression outside of the person who has them. That is, we can only express compassion when we have empathy for the needs of other people. Anyone can claim to be a person of love, but until we demonstrate our ability to love in relation to another person, we have not shown that we are people guided by love. Jesus said, "I give you a new commandment: Love one another; as I have loved you, that you also love one another. By this all will know that you are my disciples, if you have love for one another" (John 13:34-35).

Chapter Three

Misconceptions About Tithing

Bottom Line Up Front: The argument against the tithe as an Old Testament principle ignores its spiritual purpose.

Jesse Wisnewski described the tithing debate as two competing commandments: "Christians are commanded to tithe or Christians are commanded to be generous."[22] I think Wisnewski captured the debate correctly, but, like everyone else who has broached this topic, he limits the discussion to these two commandments. I am not criticizing this description. I just want to point out that while I agree that he framed the issue correctly, he did so in the traditional approach in how tithing has been discussed over the past few decades. Neither position is correct because the Bible does not present tithe and generosity as contrary commandments. The most correct way to understand the difference in emphasis is in the expectations that God has of the church in contrast to the expectations of the law. Let me expand.

---

[22] Jesse Wisnewski. El diezmo y la Biblia. https://get.tithe.ly/blog/106-bible-scriptures-about-giving. Enero de 2020.

The law prohibited stealing, but the law never stopped a single thief from stealing his neighbor's property. The commandment attempted to curve the human inclination to do harm to others, but it did not have any power against the appetites of the flesh. The law prohibited something that was common in a sinful world. So the commandments were written from a negative perspective, such as, "you shall not kill and you shall not steal," to highlight the sinful inclinations of the heart and to give the society at large the capacity to punish the guilty.

In the New Testament the commandments are from a positive perspective. When Christ left us his two commandments, he was saying that his commandments appealed to a higher law, which is the law that comes from God's image in us or from the law of the conscience. When we are guided by the law of love, which is also the law of the Spirit, we do not need an external law to guide our decisions.

Similarly, the tithe that came before the law had a different motivational force and purpose than the requirements of the law. Gratefulness is the primary motivation for the tithe. God established the tithe as the instrument that breaks the shackles with which greed had bound us. If we notice, the Ten Commandments include a rejection of greed, but they say nothing about tithing. In this book I propose that tithing is the antidote that remedies greed.

In the New Testament, we can add, the call to generosity is not a contradiction against tithing. On the contrary. Generosity is a call for us to go beyond tithing, in the same way that loving your neighbor goes beyond not stealing from others. With tithing we break the vicious cycle of love for money. With generosity we enter the realm of God's grace. The New Testament calls believers to do two things regarding tithe and offerings: to sow abundantly and to be generous with their harvest.

As you already know, I don't think tithing and generosity are contradictory or even competing positions. Since tithing measures people's level of greed, once we have overcome greed, giving generously will naturally follow. Let me say that we can preach generosity until we fall exhausted to the ground, but if believers do not overcome greed, I assure you that people who love money will never be generous.

I have pointed out that greed is a spiritual deficiency since it does not reflect a spirit of grace. But we can know how much progress we have made against greed by using tithing as our measure. Let's say, for example, that a person commits himself to Christ and joins a church. During his membership class, he understands that God was extremely generous in sending Jesus to die for our sins, and the new Christian concludes that he will give twenty percent of his income to the Lord. This person does not need a lengthy process to overcome greed. In his gratitude for Jesus's sacrifice, he came to that conclusion on his own. This person does not need long speeches for him to consider tithing as his Christian responsibility because this person has already won the battle against the love of money. Of course, this is just an illustration that I have never witnessed in church in the last sixty years, but you understand my point.

My experience has been the complete opposite of the previous example. Almost every new Christian I've known resists tithing. They don't understand or have no interest in giving more than they absolutely have to for a variety of reasons. Some new believers fear the pastor will use their tithe to buy ice cream or a new car. Whatever their reasons, it is not important. The important thing is that people always have reasons to avoid the tithe.

Breaking the cycle of greed is a process that requires different periods of time for different people because the natural instinct of the flesh is self-centeredness. Some people quickly overcome the love of money, but others can take years attending church complaining about leaving a twenty dollars offering. In my experience, Christians who tithe rarely complain, but those who give less than the tenth often complain about everything. Some believers don't even realize that churches pay their electricity bill with the donations from their faithful members. And without the offerings of the faithful, the churches cannot keep their doors open, but I digress.

Once we understand the spiritual meaning of tithing, we can also understand that tithing is a process that moves believers toward a generous and abundant life. Tithing is like a babysitter we need until we learn to walk by ourselves. For example, when I was a teenager I did some work with my school, and when it was time to tithe, I calculated the amount I had to give up to the penny. I certainly didn't want to give more than I had to, but I felt it was my Christian duty to give my tithes to my church. Once I became an adult, with a real job, and with a family, I tithed without having to calculate how much I had to give. Tithing was normal for me. Once I became an adult, say around twenty years old, I have always given more than what the tithe requires, to this day. Since I know that I always give generously, I don't even have to think about tithing, nor do I have to calculate how much I have to give.

I believe God wants Christians to move from being selfish lovers of money to a generous life that leads us to experience God's grace in abundance. I do not think the dichotomy that sets tithing and generous giving as opposite or contradictory is adequate. In fact, it is an artificially imposed tension. Presenting the tithe and generous giving as competing alternatives has done more harm than good. It has created more confusion than clarity.

It is unnecessary to see tithing and generosity as two opposing views. I suggest that generosity is the goal of the tithe, as Jesus was the goal of the law. The law was not bad, but we are bad. The law was good, but we are sinners. The tithe is good, but we are lovers of money and resist being generous. We start with the tithe to break the cycle of greed and end with generosity to be more like the Good Samaritan. I am convinced that tithing achieves the goal of making us more generous.

On the next few pages, I want to answer several common objections against the tithe. Let's take a look at some of them.

But, Isn't Tithing an Old Testament Thing?

One school of thought says that the Old Testament laws have no application to the church, and they are partly right. The Old Testament legal system was designed to guide the nation of Israel to the coming of the Messiah. The Mosaic law was never intended to be permanent, and when the Lord Jesus died for our sins, he fulfilled all the requirements of lay, and it became obsolete.

This perspective includes tithing as just another Old Testament institution therefore, tithing was repealed along with the rest of the law once the New Testament era began. This position basically says that the application of Old Testament principles to the church is limited to the illustrations and examples it provides. I do not agree with this position for two reasons.

First Reason: This position establishes an artificial separation between the Old and New Testaments, as it relates to God's character. Clearly, there is a distinction between the application of the law of Moses, as the rule of life in Israel, and the transformation produced by the cross of Christ, as manifested in the life of the church. I agree that Jesus fulfilled all the requirements of the law with his death. This also means that the law demanded the death penalty for the sin of Adam, with his death, Christ fulfilled that requirement. When Jesus fulfilled the requirements of the law, the law ceased and took its place in history. It is here that I want to make a very important distinction.

The Old Testament contains truths that go beyond the Mosaic law. For example, the Melchizedek priesthood was revealed in Genesis 14, which is in the Old Testament, but his priesthood was not removed in the New Testament because Jesus himself assumed the Melchizedek priesthood as an eternal priesthood. The book of Hebrews declared this priesthood as superior to the priesthood of Aaron. This example is one of many that indicate that there are Old Testament principles that are as valid today as they were in the past. What disappeared with the death of Christ were all the rites associated with the life of Israel, especially those associated with animal sacrifices and all the ceremonial practices of the nation (Col. 3:16-23). The apostle Paul, specifically, declared that the rites and ceremonies of the law have no effect in the church.

It is important to note that tithing is not on the list of Old Testament practices that were abrogated by the cross or by the New Testament writers. This aspect is significant because the tithe, like the Melchizedek priesthood, pre-existed the coming of the law and continues to be in effect after the law.

Reason Two: I am not in the anti-tithe group because I believe the Bible, as a whole, has the broader purpose of revealing God's character and the human condition. The centrality of God's character in biblical revelation makes the law an element of God's revelation, and not the central aspect of that revelation. I do not intend to discount the importance of the law. I am simply saying that the Mosaic law provided the context for God's revelation, but it is not, in and of itself, the entirety of God's character.

So while the law guided Israel to the cross, the greatest meaning of the law was not to divide the character of God between the Old and New Testaments. The revelation of God's character is consistent, regardless of whether it appears in the Old or New. Both wills provide the context for the revelation of God's character, and the character of God is consistent on both sides of the cross. Therefore, fighting greed was as necessary in the Old Testament as it is still in the New, and the tithe is the instrument God designed to accomplish this purpose.

Another expert group claims that the entire Bible applies to Christians because the entire Bible represents the revelation of God's character. Propose to you that the only aspects of the Old Testament that do not apply to the church are those that were abolished by Christ on the cross. The Ten Commandments are as good today as it was when Moses wrote it in that they are still a reflection of the sinful nature.

However, the Commandments are inoperative as motivators for righteousness. God never intended them for that purpose. The cross and Jesus's love motivates us. People remain under condemnation because they cannot meet the requirements of justice that God demands. When Jesus fulfilled the requirements of the law, he abolished in his flesh the penalty imposed by sin. And we who have received the grace of God through Christ do not have to suffer the eternal death sentence imposed by law. That said, I affirm that the revelation of the character of God in the Old Testament is as effective today as it was then.

One of the basic foundations of biblical interpretation is that the principles of the Old and New Testaments apply to all believers of all ages, as long as they have not been adjusted or become obsolete because they are directly related to the religious ritual practices of Israel. For example: all ceremonial laws, such as animal sacrifices, the celebration of new moons, and weekly and annual Saturdays, are not requirements for the church (Col. 2:16-19). The apostle Paul clarified this point:

> Therefore let no one judge you in food or drink, or in regard to feast days, a new moon, or Sabbath days, all of which are a shadow of what is to come; but the body is of Christ (Col. 2:16-19).

The church has no obligation, and the apostle Paul did not expect us to keep the Jewish Sabbath. All the ceremonial laws lost their value when Christ came. The ceremonial and sacrificial laws were a shadow of what was to come. Once the real has arrived, Jesus, there was no need to continue living in the shadow. Christ is our Sabbath, and we do not need a ceremonial rest, even though it is found in the original Ten Commandments. Christ is our salvation and we don't need any more superficial sacrifices or rituals that have no spiritual value. He is our peace, and we don't need any more peace offerings. There is no longer a need for animal sacrifices because God is satisfied with the payment that Christ presented to the Father for our sins. This is a basic and simple principle of interpretation.

The tithe is different from the other ceremonial laws of the Old Testament for a primary reason. The tithe was established 450 years before the Mosaic Law and serves to evaluate the greed of the human heart. The fact that the tithe preceded the law would suffice as an eternal principle, but when we acknowledge the spiritual problem created by greed, there is no question of its importance to all believers in all ages.

Therefore, I maintain that the restrictions of the law do not apply to the tithe. We cannot forget that the Abrahamic covenant was established before the Law, and the Law that came after it did not invalidate the covenant. Paul made reference to this point when he declared that "the covenant previously ratified by God towards Christ, the law that came four hundred and thirty years later, does not abrogate it, to invalidate the promise" (Gal. 3:17). The fact that the Abrahamic covenant included tithe is not in question because Abraham, the recipient of the covenant, gave the tithe to Melchizedek after receiving his blessing. When Abraham tithed to Melchizedek, he accepted that *El-Elyon*, who was the same God that Melchizedek worshiped, as his only Lord.

But, Didn't Abraham Only Tithe Once?

Another objection against the tithe is that Abraham's example is not normative for the New Testament church because he only tithed once. Let me share some thoughts why I disagree with this assertion. From my perspective, Abraham is normative, but not because he continued to tithe frequently. The example of the patriarch is normative because his tithe to Melchizedek established the pattern of tithing to one with a higher rank. The writer of Hebrews declared that the superior, Melchizedek, blessed the inferior, Abraham (Heb. 7:7). I agree that Abraham did not establish the pattern of weekly tithes to a local church, but this is not how biblical patterns develop. Abraham's action showed Melchizedek that the patriarch had conquered greed.

The pattern of conquering greed is valid for the church today because we too have to break the cycle of greed if God is going to expand our influence.

If the objection is that Abraham did not go to church every Sunday to tithe, then the objectors are looking at this event from the wrong perspective. When Abraham met Melchizedek, this was a symbolic event between the representative of God and the man with whom God would affirm the everlasting covenant a chapter later. Not only that, but Melchizedek blessed Abraham and Abraham in turn tithed to the high priest. These two acts, the blessing and the tithes, were prerequisites for the covenant affirmation that took place in Genesis 15:9-21. No one should think that these events were random coincidences and that God did not play a role in organizing the meeting between Melchizedek and Abraham.

When the high priest of the Most High God blessed Abraham, he acted as the human representative who ratified the covenant that God would make with Abraham. Please read the following carefully. Since we have no reference to tithing prior to this meeting, the only way Abraham could have known about the tithe was if God had revealed it to him. By revelation I don't mean that an angel came from heaven and convinced Abraham to give the ten percent of his loot to the high priest. That revelation could have been as simple as Abraham, after receiving the blessing, asked himself, what would be the proper response I should give to the High Priest of God? After considering his answer, Abraham concluded that ten percent was the proper answer.

The biblical writer recorded the moment and the tithe became the natural response of Abraham's descendants to receive God's grace. We are sons and daughters of Abraham through faith and participants in the Abrahamic covenant and, as such, we must respond to God's blessing just as Abraham did. This event was not a routine encounter, and Abraham's offering indicated that God has the prerogative of the tithe, because there is no other God like him.

One last clarification on Abraham's tithe. Those who use this objection have said that there is no record that Abraham has tithed again. Very true. Similarly, I can say that there is no indication that the patriarch did not visit Melchizedek regularly. After all, they lived in the same region. The fact is, there is no evidence as to whether or not Abraham re-tithed. So I think this statement is an argument from silence that is not persuasive. However, we have plenty of evidence in Israel's history that God's people continued to use tithing as their primary method of supporting God's mission through the Tent of Meeting and later through the Temple. Furthermore, the author of the book of Hebrews argues that when Abraham presented his tithe to Melchizedek, the Levites, who entered the scene more than six hundred years later, were included in Abraham's tithe, and yet the law required the Levites to also offer a tithe from the tithe. We were included in Abraham's tithe as well, but like the Levites, we are required to bring the tithe to the God's house.

I will conclude by saying that the tithe is not a financial transaction between God and us or a tax to support the government, although many have used these two terms interchangeably in reference to Israel's tithe. On the contrary. The tithe is a spiritual act where we express our gratitude to God in return for his grace and blessings. When we keep the tithe we are rejecting the fact that Abraham recognized Melchizedek, and by extension the Lord, has the right to receive the tithe in response to our blessings in Christ. By the way, when Abraham tithed to Melchizedek, he was symbolically tithing to Jesus.

But, Wasn't the Tithe to Sustain the Levites?

During the dispensation of the law, the tithe supported the Levites as God's representative for their temple service. They were the conduit to receive the tithe to test the character of Israel. God's purpose has not changed. There still needs to be food in God's house. Paul declared that "a worker deserves his wages" (1 Tim. 5:18). The source of Christian workers' wages is the tithes and offerings of the faithful. Obviously, Christian pastors today, like the Levites of yesteryear, receive their livelihood from the generous gifts of the church. Therefore, the Old Testament model, as a practical matter, works for the church today as well. But we cannot forget that the main purpose of the tithe is spiritual.

But, How Much Should we Tithe?

When I was in high school, a long time ago, I had the highest math score in our graduating class college exam (the equivalent of the SAT today) in the entire island of Puerto Rico. I scored 799 out of a possible 800 score. I still remember that ten percent of 100 is 10, and ten percent of 1,000 is 100. I can keep going up, but two examples suffice.

The previous question muddies up the tithe by adding all the taxes the kings imposed on the people. Based on my math experience in high school I would suggest that the answer to the question of how much people should we tithe today is easy: we tithe ten percent of our increase. Remember that once we have overcome the greed barrier, the tenth is only our starting point, even though God is not requiring us to go further. God is satisfied with the tenth, but he knows that once we have overcome greed, the ten percent is the minimum we will give in response to God's grace and our salvation.

Some scholars have suggested that we cannot know how much we should tithe because in Israel the people tithed more than the tenth. To that I say, so what? The tithe is still ten percent, and the fact that some of Israel's kings or high priests taxed the people more than ten percent, does not mean that the tithe had lost its effectiveness. The principle of the tithe is based on Abraham, not the law.

Additionally, those who are unsure as to how much they should tithe, based on the Mosaic Law's model, they could start with eleven percent as a sign that they had broken their love and addiction to money.

But, Wasn't Jesus Still Under the Law When he Affirmed the Tithe?

Of all the objections against tithing this is the least consistent. If we discard everything Jesus said while he was "still under the law," then we would take nothing of what he said seriously. We cannot minimize the teachings of Jesus because everything he said has eternal value, and eternal principles are not tied to the time when they were revealed. Let me tell you something that Jesus said before the beginning of the church age. He said:

> Do not lay up for yourselves treasures on earth, where moth and rust corrupt, and where thieves undermine and steal; [20] but make yourselves treasures in heaven, where neither moth nor rust corrupts, and where thieves do not undermine nor steal. [21]For where your treasure is, there your heart will also be (Matt. 5:21-23).

If the principle that all that Christ affirmed before his death does not apply to the church, then we would have to conclude that Christians can keep their hearts focused on their earthly treasures. Obviously, this would be a mistake of gigantic proportions. The main problem with this objection to tithing is that it limits the principle of Jesus being under the law to tithes and nothing else. Jesus's teaching was consistent. Love of money is an obstacle that prevents a spiritually healthy relationship with God. That our treasure should be in heaven is true no matter when Jesus said so.

I am of the opinion that everything Jesus taught, affirmed, or endorsed, applies to the church age. We must remember the Gospel writers did not include all the words or deeds of the Lord, but practically all of the teachings of Christ were before his crucifixion. That is, Jesus was under the law throughout his ministry, except the forty days after the resurrection. As far as I know, no one has preached that we must discard everything that Jesus taught before the cross, except for the tithe, that is. The gospel writers, inspired by the Holy Spirit, included all the events and words that they considered most relevant to the Christian faith. And as the writers may have noticed, they included the claim that Jesus tithed. Let's read the relevant passage here.

> "Woe to you, scribes and Pharisees, hypocrites! For you tithe mint and dill and cumin and have neglected the weightier matters of the law: justice and mercy and faithfulness. These you ought to have done, without neglecting the others. [24] You blind guides, straining out a gnat and swallowing a camel! (Matt. 23:23-24).

Let me make three observations related to this passage. First, although Jesus made the tithe inferior to justice and mercy, he did not say that this minor obligation was optional. In his own words, he said, "This [justice, mercy, and faith] needed to be done, while still doing the other [tithing]" (Matt. 23:23b). Jesus did not say that once they showed mercy they could ignore the tithe because it did not have the same level of importance as justice, mercy, and faith. We cannot read the passage in this way because then we would spoil the importance of the comparison, which Jesus used, precisely, to criticize the Pharisees for being selective in their obedience.

Second, Jesus spoke of the tithe as the norm for believers. We must remember the disciples were present when the Lord said these words and they must have understood what Christ's intentions were. In the way that Jesus introduced the contrast, he was assuming that the tithe was not a controversial issue at all. On the contrary. The context suggests that tithing is the entry level of obedience to God. Christ's intention was to communicate that justice, mercy, and faith should have been as natural and common to them as tithing.

Finally, when Jesus said the Pharisees "strained the gnat, and swallowed the camel," he did not imply that swallowing mosquitoes was acceptable. In other words, the message from Jesus was that it was necessary to strain the mosquito, but it was more important to also strain the camel. Jesus was challenging the Pharisees' legalistic that cherry picked what commandments to obey and which ones they wanted to ignore. If the Pharisees were going to swallow something, they should have swallowed the mosquito. But we cannot interpret the contrast as an endorsement for swallowing mosquitoes. Or, put another way—doing justice does not mean that we can ignore the tithe.

The idea that Jesus affirmed the tithe because he was under the law is a silly idea (Gal. 4:4). This is like saying that Christ did not understand in impact his words could have on his audience or that Jesus was confused on whether his words could carry weight beyond the cross. We all know Jesus challenged the common understanding of the law more than any. When Jesus healed the paralytic on a Sabbath, experts in the law strongly criticized him (Jn. 5:1-17). According to the experts of the law Jesus should not have healed this man on the Sabbath. While it can be argued that they had misinterpreted the law, the fact is that Jesus did not debate their understanding of the law. He simply challenged their contradiction between mercy and the law.

In the same way that Jesus clarified the true intentions of the law on numerous occasions, he could have made a similar clarification without using the tithe. Or, he could have said: you heard that it was said that they had to tithe, but I tell you that tithing is not necessary as long as people give with joy. Jesus spent a lot of time correcting the most common and serious misunderstandings about the law, but when the tithe came, he simply accepted that the Pharisees had the correct understanding.

I believe that Old Testament practices that were not intrinsically linked to the law, such as the tithe, and that were still in practice, Jesus left in place. Let me close this section by saying that the fact Jesus said something before the cross is not an indication that his words became inoperative after Pentecost. Best interpretive practice is to look at the teachings of Jesus from the perspective of how they define God's character, and not from the perspective of whether Jesus might have said something before his death.

But, What About Paul's Letter to the Corinthians?

Let me quote Paul's statement to the Corinthians.

6 The point is this: whoever sows sparingly will also reap sparingly, and whoever sows bountifully will also reap bountifully. **7** Each one must give as he has decided in his heart, not reluctantly or under compulsion, for God loves a cheerful giver (2 Cor. 9:6-7).

I want to start my discussion in this section by commenting on what Paul did not say. He did not say: in the Old Testament the people of Israel practiced tithing, but the tithe's effectiveness died with the law and it became inoperative for the church age. I believe any argument from silence is suspect, but we cannot argue that the tithe is obsolete without any evidence to that effect. The reality is that there not one solitary passage in the New Testament that dismissed the effectiveness of the tithe. But there are several New Testament passages, including Jesus's words, that support the tithe.

In this passage, the apostle's focus was a special offering the Corinthian church had promised Paul to support his ministry (2 Cor. 9:5). While Paul encouraged the church to give cheerfully, the text does not suggest that the apostle was establishing a new method for giving in the universal Church. He was simply emphasizing the Christian duty to be of good cheer in supporting God's work through Paul. Since the church had promised him an offering to support his ministry, he was giving them a heads up that some brothers from Macedonian would be coming by to collect the offering. It is also instructive that the apostle echoed Jesus's teachings about generosity, which is the attitude of the spiritually transformed mind. But as I have argued throughout this book, generosity is the natural outcome of overcoming greed which can only happen when we are faithful with the tithe.

I think it is poor hermeneutics to use this text as the basis for establishing the doctrine of "giving with joy" as a replacement of the tithe. This is especially true because Paul did not even mention the tithe once. Paul's specific purpose in this passage was limited to reminding the church of the special offering they had promised him to support his missionary efforts.

The apostle Paul told the Corinthians that their generous gift would result in them being "enriched in every way to be generous in every way." With these words the apostle was affirming God's promise to meet all the church's needs if they generously supported his ministry. The apostle added that "the ministry of this service not only supplies what is lacking to the saints, but also abounds in many thanksgivings to God" (2 Cor. 9:12). What ministry was the apostle referring to? Obviously, to Paul's missionary ministry, and not to the obligations of the local church to pay rent, electricity and pastoral wages. Let me repeat once again that the only clearly defined method of giving in the church is the tithe and the voluntary offerings of the saints. As Christians, once we have conquered greed, we can give more generously.

I think it is a hermeneutical mistake to use Paul's request for a specific offering and turn it into a rejection of tithing. I suggest Jesus's message about giving generously to receive an overflowing blessing, and Paul's teaching on the law of sowing and reaping in this passage, does not in any way mean that tithing is no longer operative. I think the opposite is true. It is impossible to read this passage without reflecting on Malachi's message when the Lord said, "bring tithing to the storehouse so that there is food in my house, and I will open the windows of heaven and pour out a blessing until there is no more need" (Mal. 3:10). I assure you that there is no contradiction in these three sentences:

- "I will pour out a blessing until there is no more need" (Mal. 3:10)
- "Running over, will be pour into your lap" (Lk. 6:38).
- "Whoever sows bountifully, will also receive bountifully" (2 Cor. 9: 6).

These three phrases are three different ways to say the same thing. God will bless his people when we honor him with our tithes and offerings. But the reader must remember that the tithe is the basis of all three statements.

This passage is not a pattern similar to Abraham for a main reason. Abraham chose the tithe in response to Melchizedek's blessing before God confirmed the covenant with the patriarch. That event signaled Abraham's recognition that Melchizedek was entitled to receive the tithe of all his spoils of war. In Paul's situation, he specifically stated that the Corinthian church had made a promise to send him an offering to support his ministry, something the churches of Philippi and Macedonia had repeatedly done. To encourage the church in its effort to fulfill its offering promise, Paul had been "anticipating" the church's willingness to support his ministry (2 Cor. 9:3). Paul, in preparation to send the Macedonians to collect the offering, sent a letter to the church ahead of time to make sure they were prepared with their offering for the ministry.

Today's Christians start with the tithe and from there we increase to give generously, as an act of thanksgiving for the goodness of God. Paul's message is relevant to the church because he reaffirmed the law of sowing and reaping, when he said that "he who sows bountifully will also reap bountifully" (2 Cor. 9:6). But this principle is related to the law of seedtime and harvest, and it does not deny the tithe. The members of Corinth were to give to Paul's ministry as each "had decided in his heart, not reluctantly or under compulsion, because God loves a joyful giver" (2 Cor. 9:7).

The principle of giving with joy was true about the Corinthian offering to Paul, and it also applies to the attitude that all Christians should have in all actions, and not just in giving. This is my point here: while giving with joy is a principle that reveals our generosity, Paul was not replacing tithing with "giving with joy." This was a special offering that Paul received, probably, once a year. Therefore, although giving with gratitude and joy is a pattern for the church, the apostle did not say the tithe was now obsolete.

This pattern can also be seen with the Philippian church. The apostle was very grateful that the Philippians was the only church that had continued to support his ministry, even after Paul left Macedonia. Read it with me.

> [14] Yet it was kind of you to share my trouble. [15] And you Philippians yourselves know that in the beginning of the gospel, when I left Macedonia, no church entered into partnership with me in giving and receiving, except you only. [16] Even in Thessalonica you sent me help for my needs once and again. [17] Not that I seek the gift, but I seek the fruit that increases to your credit (Phil. 4:14-16).

As you can see, the apostle expressed his appreciation for the generosity of the Philippian church. They had been the only ones who had sent money to different places. Paul was so impressed with the ministry of the Philippians that he said that offerings were sent to him "even in Thessalonica." The phrase "even in Thessalonica" probably means that he did not need offerings while he was there, or that it took a great effort to bring the offering to that church. Either way, the apostle was grateful for his financial support.

One last word in this section. Christians must be joyful and generous givers. But joy and generosity are conditions of the heart that can only find expression after people have conquered their greed, not before. Therefore, the perceived contradiction between tithe and joyful giving is an unnecessary controversy.

Conclusion

Some believers say they have survived as Christians without giving the tithe. Some of these Christians even believe that tithing is a nefarious church plan to appropriate their money. If that's what some people thinks, that's their option. My purpose in this book was not to tell believers what to do with what they think it's their money. I simply wanted to present the theological requirements God has revealed, if we are to honor him as the Lord of our lives. This means that if God is God, and if this God has spoken, then what he has said is of extreme importance. Christians everywhere know that God cannot entrust us with more responsibility than we can handle. As such, if we cannot manage our finances well, then, God cannot entrust to us the finances of the Church. If God cannot trust us, how can we expect that he will expand our territory of influence?

This is my point: God's principles for financial success work 100% of the time. However, the reason many Christians struggle financially is the result of their failure to earned God's trust to receive the benefits of his generous blessings. Until we have shown that we can manage our own check books effectively, and this includes the tithe, God cannot trust us to manage his books. Think about it. If God blesses people without being spiritually and emotionally prepared to manage the money in the church, they will sell their souls to the devil, which is the point of the rich ruler of the story I mentioned at the beginning of our journey.

Not many of us, who love our children, would give them a sharp knife to play with. No one would do such a thing because most people know that children are not mature enough to handle sharp knives and they will get hurt. That is exactly God's point. Having more money than we can handle is like giving a sharp blade to our children, and the Lord knows this and protects us.

When people steal from God the windows of heaven are closed (Mal. 3:8). This means that our ability to make wise, divinely inspired decisions will be affected. At that time, all it gives a person is the wisdom of the world, and we know that the Bible describes the wisdom of the world as foolishness in the presence of God. The most common mistake we make is to think that when the Bible talks about money, God is talking about gold and silver or any other material that is used for financial exchange.

Most people, including many Christians, do not understand that when the Bible talks about money, it is using metaphor to describe the condition of the human heart. Money exposes our level of greed or reveals whether we have grown to live beyond the love of money. Let me clarify that overcoming the love of money does not mean that we do not need money to survive. On the contrary, it means that we are not controlled by its corrupting influence. We should never forget Paul's words to Timothy that "love of money is the cause of all kinds of evil." That is, if we are going to fulfill God's purpose for our lives, our souls need to be healed from the disease of greed, and tithing is the divine instrument that helps us conquer this enemy.

Two Problems

I want to discuss two problems with the Church today and how we understand the tithe. I use the word problem because these two attitudes prevent the church from flourishing financially.

112

The first problem is that, although the church has accepted Jesus as Lord, most Christians do not take seriously what God says. This is not a new problem. The people of Israel did not take God seriously either. Let's take a look at an example.

> ³ For six years you shall sow your field, and for six years you shall prune your vineyard and gather in its fruits, ⁴ but in the seventh year there shall be a Sabbath of solemn rest for the land, a Sabbath to the Lord. You shall not sow your field or prune your vineyard. ⁵ You shall not reap what grows of itself in your harvest or gather the grapes of your undressed vine. It shall be a year of solemn rest for the land. (Lev. 25:3-5).

The reader may rightly ask what this passage has to do with the tithe? Dear brothers, this passage is an illustration of how the people of Israel ignored God's call to follow the annual Sabbath commandments. The Lord told them that if they submitted to his requirements, the Lord Himself would meet all their financial needs. But the people refused to obey God. Either they did not think or believe that God knew how to keep score, or they did not realize that their past actions were going to influence their present consequences. Listen to the words that the prophet Jeremiah proclaimed to the people for ignoring the command regarding annual Sabbaths:

> ¹¹ This whole land shall become a ruin and a waste, and these nations shall serve the king of Babylon seventy years. ¹² Then after seventy years are completed, I will punish the king of Babylon and that nation, the land of the Chaldeans, for their iniquity, declares the Lord, making the land an everlasting waste (Jer. 25:11-12).

> ²⁰ He took into exile in Babylon those who had escaped from the sword, and they became servants to him and to his sons until the establishment of the kingdom of Persia, ²¹ to fulfill the word of the Lord by the mouth of Jeremiah, until the land had enjoyed its Sabbaths. All the days that it lay desolate it kept Sabbath, to fulfill seventy years (2 Chr. 36:21-22).

Jeremiah predicted that Judah would serve Babylon for 70 years (Jer. 25:11; 29:10). In the year 605 a. C., Judah was taken captive to

Babylon according to Jeremiah's prophecy. Then, the book of Daniel recorded the end of the seventy-year captivity when Cyrus invaded and conquered Babylon in 535 b. C. These events could only mean that for 490 years, or from the time of the Judges, Israel ignored God's command that the land had to rest for a full year after six years of sowing and harvesting (2 Chr. 36:21; Jer. 25:11; Jer. 25:12; Jer. 29:10; Dan. 9: 2; Zech. 1:12; Zech. 7: 5).

Just as the people of Israel ignored God's commandments regarding the annual Sabbaths, the Church today ignores God's call to support the proclamation of the Gospel with our tithes and offerings. I recognize that many faithful Christians provide a great deal of support for the church. But I also recognize that we have not even begun to scratch the surface regarding our giving obligations. The people of Israel did not believe God really expected the land to rest every seven years. Most likely, they were convinced that it was unrealistic for God to expect them to go a full year without working. Christians today have the same attitude: God cannot expect us to give ten percent of our income to the church. He knows perfectly well that we have to pay for our new cars. He knows we need two 50-inch televisions, and God knows very well that we have to take our families to Disney World this year. So, we tell ourselves that God can't be serious about this tithe thing. This is so antiquated for this modern world!

Refusing to believe and trust God are the main reasons only fifteen to twenty percent of Christians consistently give to their churches. This unspoken rebellion also means that eighty percent of Christians do not give with any consistency, if at all. An article in *NP Source*[23] described the offering habits in today's church:

- 37% of regular church attendees and Evangelicals don't give to their churches at all

---

[23] NP Source. The ultimate list of charitable giving statistics for 2018.
https://nonprofitssource.com/online-giving-statistics/

- Faithful tithers average give between 11% and 20% of their incomes to their churches
- The average annual donations from American Christians to their churches is $200 a year, which is less than .05% of the average income
- 5% of Christians in the United States give 60% of all tithes and offerings (without this faithful group, all the churches in the United States would be bankrupt. Conversely, if 5% give 60%, then, 95% of Christians give the other 40%.)
- 80% of Christians only give 2% of their income
- 99% of the people who make more than $75K do not tithe
- People who earn between $10k and $20k give an average of 2.3% of their income

As you can see, the church's failure to overcome the cycle of greed has left the church financially bankrupt. It's no wonder that so many pastors have to resort to sales tricks to survive. The same people who don't tithe complain that the shepherds are selling soup and macaroni and cheese to balance the budget. I think the church in America has been faithful with the tithe, and we are on the verge of God sending us into financial exile.

We all know most people in the United States are in debt. I believe that our failure to overcome greed, in the midst of a consumer society, is the main reason Christians spend more than they earn. The people of Israel spent seventy years in Babylon because God had to collect the debt of the annual Sabbaths the people owed him, and God always collects his debts. For 490 years Israel ignored God's command regarding the annual Sabbaths. Similarly, today's church is in financial crisis because we abandoned God's model to give and break the cycle of love of money, and we have invented all kinds of excuses to avoid the tithe. In fact, we have become so smart at avoiding tithing that we even say that giving one-point-two percent of our income is considered generous. We are in a situation where we cannot enjoy what we earn because we are wasting our money on credit card interest and expensive toys that we don't need. The less we give, the more we get into debt.

From an economic point of view, if Christians, individually and collectively, made the decision to get out of all debts (close credit cards and pay all the loans we have) we would be truly free to offer generously for the Lord's work. We would prosper beyond our most wildest dreams. The Bible says that "he who borrows is a slave to him who lends" (Prov. 22:7). Christians are enslaved, not to other Christians, but to the world. Until recently, about 50 years ago, the United States was the world's leading nation in lending to others. Today the United States borrows more money than any other nation in the world, and with an external debt of more than twenty-two trillion dollars, one day our financial system will collapse.

Our national debt is so large that not even the antichrist wants to take it over. There was a time when Christians were not so indebted, and neither was the nation. But when the church began to bow to the gods of greed and secularism, the nation also turned away from God, and as a result, our greed made us a nation of debtors. We are now slaves to foreign governments, and the church has adopted the same bad habit as the nation.

The second problem that most Christians have is that we do not understand how inflexible and extensive the law of sowing and reaping is. By this I do not mean that I have knowledge that other Christians do not have. Most Christians know that God created this world as an agricultural system. That's not the problem. Our failure is that we do not trust that God's system really works as he designed it. Imagine being a farmer who sows his seed, but who does not believe the land can reproduce the seed as God designed it. As I mentioned earlier, in God's world everything works in a process of seedtime and harvest. Every tree, plant, fruit, root, animal, and person works in a cycle of seedtime and harvest. There is nothing in this world that has life that does not depend on the cycle of time of seeds and harvest. Read with me some verses that talk about this agricultural system.

[28] And God blessed them. And God said to them, "Be fruitful and multiply and fill the earth and subdue it, and have dominion over the fish of the sea and over the birds of the heavens and over every living thing that moves on the earth." [29] And God said, "Behold, I have given you every plant yielding seed that is on the face of all the earth, and every tree with seed in its fruit. You shall have them for food (Gen. 1:28-29).

[17] And to Adam he said, "Because you have listened to the voice of your wife and have eaten of the tree of which I commanded you, 'You shall not eat of it,' cursed is the ground because of you; in pain you shall eat of it all the days of your life; [18] thorns and thistles it shall bring forth for you; and you shall eat the plants of the field. [19] By the sweat of your face you shall eat bread, till you return to the ground, for out of it you were taken; for you are dust, and to dust you shall return (Gen. 3:17-19).

[7] Do not be deceived: God is not mocked, for whatever one sows, that will he also reap. (Gal. 6:7)

Of all the principles that Christians must learn in their lives about generosity and accountability, the law of sowing and reaping is the most important. There are five seasons in this process: (1) plowing — preparing the ground, (2) sowing — putting the seed into fertile soil, (3) watering — making sure there is enough water to give life to the seed, (4) growth — the secret of germination that God created, and (5) harvest — the time of gathering the fruits. If Christians want to increase the efficiency of their finances, we must generously sow our financial seeds in the Kingdom of God. It may take a while for our finances to catch up with our needs, but eventually God will open the windows of heaven and the blessings will begin to flow freely.

Two Solutions

The first solution for God's blessings to flow to our churches is to develop a global vision. Having a global vision does not mean that every small church in our neighborhoods will focus on sending missionaries to China and Pakistan. A global vision means that the vision is so big that we can only achieve it with God's intervention.

Failure to present and articulate a clear vision of the ministry has two possible negative consequences. First, we cannot expect people to follow us if we do not know where we are going. Second, we cannot financial support if our vision is too small. It is important to note that God will bless our vision at the level necessary to achieve it. That is, if we have a vision that does not require God's intervention, such as feeding the hungry, then God does not need to get involved. All we need to feed the hungry is a car with and a pot of rice. We can drive under a bridge, find the hungry and give them some food. However, if the vision includes providing kitchens, cooking utensils, and empowering people to prepare their own meals, ten, we will need God's intervention. The question is not whether feeding the hungry is a good mission. The question is whether the vision is large enough to require the miraculous hand of God.

I must add here that God does not bless buildings or good intentions. I believe God blesses people with a vision that fits the mission that Christ commissioned to us to make disciples of all nations. I encourage all pastors to redefine their church vision in a way that is greater than anything they can do. In this way God has to intervene so that the mission is accomplished.

A clear vision is essential to encourage members to give generously. No one wants to give support to a building. But most people will not hesitate to give to a righteous cause. The mission of our churches has to be the mission of God's kingdom. Until it is, the vision of our churches is too small. Remember that people should be able to easily memorize and repeat the vision.

The second solution is related to personal and corporate finances. One statistic says that of all the churches that close their doors in the United States every year, 80% of them fail as a result of poor financial decisions. We need to train all church leaders in the finances of the kingdom of God to ensure the survival of their churches. Many problems can influence the life and survival of a particular church, but financial mismanagement is at the top of the list. Let me make three specific suggestions for churches in this area.

First, all churches, large and small, must find a third party to manage their payroll, even if they only have one employee, such as the pastor. Without this payroll arrangement, the church is always at risk of being outside the bounds of the law.

Second, all churches must find software that enables them to make accurate financial reports on a regular basis. This type of software is not only useful in managing day-to-day financial needs, but it simplifies the reporting process in case the church has to get a mortgage or other types of money assistance.

Lastly, each church must have a written budget with categories that represent the needs of the church, such as salaries, rent or mortgage, bills, missions, benevolence and mourning, among others.

I cannot emphasize enough how important these elements are to a successful organization. These three suggestions will not guarantee that any church will prosper or survive, but without putting these three principles into action, survival becomes a more difficult task.